SHAPIN[illegible] THE HYPE

How Women Turn Technology Into Real-World Impact

CREATED BY MICHAELA HERMANS

WITH DEMET DAGDELEN, KLAUDIA CZARNECKA-KOWCUN, KATIA KOBYLINSKI MBA, EMMA DI IORIO, STEFANIA ANGIUS, DR. SIMONA JENERS, MARTA JAKAB MBA, TAMARA ZAVIŠIĆ, TIJANA ŽUNIĆ MARIĆ, SANJA BOGDANOVIĆ-DINIĆ, FRANCES PHILLIPS TAFT, JD, CIPP/E AND CIPP/US, ANNA JULI ROSENFELD, IRINA JOANNA GEBAUER, DR. MARINA ECONOMIDOU, ELISAVET KYRITSI, SANAZ JAMALZADEH, PHD, ROSALINE PAHUD DE MORTANGES, DR. PATRICIA GOODWIN-PETERS, ISAURA MARTÍNEZ.

FOREWORD BY MEGHNA SINHA

First Published in Hungary in 2025.

A CIP catalogue record for this book is available in the Hungarian National Bibliography.
ISBN: 978-615-02-5080-9

CONTENTS

PART IV: HUMAN SIGNAL

PART V: THE EDGE OF UNDERSTANDING

REFERENCES

Editor's Note

Amid the noise of AI headlines and LinkedIn fatigue, I wanted something grounded. Less noise, more practice. Focused on outcomes, collaboration, and the people doing the real work, especially the women whose leadership often goes unseen in an industry still lacking balance.

After years leading digital and AI transformation, I have seen how progress happens and how often women drive it with clarity and persistence. Many pages came together late at night with our toddler tugging at my sleeve. That is part of the story too.

When I reached out to women in AI I knew, and others I admired from afar, I did not expect the response to be this strong. Voices across industries and borders shared how they lead and what keeps them grounded in environments obsessed with newness.

Each chapter brings lived experience and lessons others can apply. These are reflections from women shaping change while managing teams, deadlines, and often families in the next room. The goal is simple: make progress real, responsible, and practical.

There is no better person to open this book than Meghna Sinha, a leading voice in responsible AI and diversity in tech. Meghna's foreword shows why these stories matter now and how they shape the future of work, leadership, and trust in AI.

– Michaela Hermans

Foreword

As an executive with 27 years of experience developing AI capabilities that have delivered business outcomes across Fortune 50 firms, I was instantly drawn to writing this foreword for a unique collaborative book featuring 20 accomplished women in technology leadership. Advocating for women has always been central to developing the highest-performing, most equitable teams and culture.

Sadly, stories of women having insightful work rejected, promotions passed over, or intellectual contributions stolen are far too common. However, these setbacks are often only the beginning of their stories. This book is a powerful collective guide from 20 women who transformed those hurdles into strategies, remaining undeterred by hype and focused on real-world outcomes.

I had an epiphany when my therapist recently explained that workplace trauma could include being undermined, ignored, or overlooked. I instantly realized this had happened throughout my career. I didn't realize this was considered trauma; I thought it was simply the tax every woman or person of minority pays in a technical career. This tax happens often unintentionally, but it continues despite professional success. This daily reality is why the stories in Shaping AI Without The Hype are so essential.

My experience navigating the peak AI hype only validated this pattern of dismissal. I encountered a new level of dismissal for practical AI capabilities that actually generate business value, even as leaders flocked to GenAI chatbots. The biggest lesson was clear: practitioners know the value of fundamental competencies even when peers ignore them in favor of new trends. We must proactively bring their expertise to the table as we reshape work alongside machines that will have agency and autonomy.

I invite you to meet these smart, accomplished women and truly immerse yourself in their lived experiences. Across these chapters, you will hear stories much like my own from women in influential roles: a CFO reflecting on her evolving role, a marketer on ChatGPT's job implications, a CHRO on the role of humanity, and an entrepreneur/CTO offering a smarter path for Europe. You will meet leaders working across healthcare, the creator economy, policy, privacy, ethics, AI, data, and product management.

We hear constantly from billionaires and investors, but not enough from real practitioners. The stories in this book reject the prevailing AI hype, focusing instead on tough issues like AI literacy, job transformation, governance, and IP protection. Each story is unique, personal, and told in the author's unwavering style. I hope these stories give you actionable insights, strategies, and guidance to shape AI in your work and life, so that, together, we can retire the concept of 'workplace trauma' as an inevitability.

- Meghna Sinha

ABOUT THE AUTHOR

Meghna Sinha is a trailblazing AI executive and strategist, currently Chief AI Officer at Kai Roses, Inc. With over 27 years of experience, she specializes in delivering responsible, enterprise-scale AI value for Fortune 50 companies, including Verizon and Target, generating over $1 billion in value. She is dedicated to the ethical and equitable advancement of the field, serving as a Distinguished Fellow with AI2030 and researching sustainable AI competency as a Senior Industry Fellow at the UC Irvine Center for Digital Transformation.

PART I: CONTEXT AS STRATEGY

Why understanding systems and causality is the new competitive edge.

ABOUT THE AUTHOR

Michaela Hermans, MBA, is a digital transformation executive with 15+ years of experience leading digital growth, enterprise transformation, and automation initiatives across global brands including Wizz Air, Nike, ING, and GrandVision.

She focuses on turning technology, data, and automation into measurable business results. Michaela also mentors women in tech and is a creator of *Women Shaping AI Without the Hype*, a collaborative book showcasing real-world female leadership driving impact through AI and transformation.

|1|

Beyond Models: Why Context is Your Only Intellectual Property

There is something magnetic about aviation. At any age, we are drawn to those bird-like machines connecting the familiar with the unknown. Whenever our 1.5-year-old spots a plane, he shouts "airplane, airplane" and when it's gone, "more airplanes."

AI sparks that same sense of wonder, opening horizons we could not have imagined. ChatGPT made it conversational. Vibe coding lets us describe ideas and prototypes appear. Now, AI agents can chain steps and interact across tools. Their true autonomy remains limited, despite the hype on social media.

But this is where the aviation parallel breaks down. Aviation achieves reliability rates of 99.9 percent [1]. According to research by MIT and BCG, fewer than one in ten generative AI pilots have scaled to deliver measurable business impact [2]. McKinsey once reported that 70 percent of digital transformation programs failed to meet their objectives, and the numbers haven't improved. If anything, the *golden rush* for AI has made the gap between promise and delivery even wider.

After 15 years leading digital transformations across banking, retail, consumer brands, and aviation, I can confirm: neither number is exaggerated. AI projects rarely crash; they fizzle. Sometimes they deliver, but rarely what was intended. And those projects never make it to LinkedIn headlines.

Aviation didn't become reliable by accident. It got there through rigorous discipline, repeated testing, and a culture that doesn't ignore failure. Every incident is examined, and the findings are built directly into how the system operates [3].

Implementing AI demands a similar level of discipline. But here's the problem: traditional software follows deterministic logic where inputs produce predictable outputs. Modern AI, by contrast, is probabilistic; it learns from data patterns rather than fixed instructions. You train behavior from data. That shift breaks many of the old assumptions about testing, deployment, and maintenance. Models will come and go. Breakthroughs arrive daily, each one overtaking the last. The technology keeps accelerating, but funnily enough, most organizations are still taxiing on the runway. That's why the real advantage no longer lies in the model itself, but in the **context** it operates in and defines.

The Model Was Ready, We Weren't

AI often arrives like a shiny new Lego set from well-meaning grandparents. The packaging is slick, and your toddler can't wait to tear it open. Then reality sets in: you walk barefoot across stray pieces, sometimes even find them in your lunchbox.

But the Lego itself is a brilliant toy. With the right baseplate and a picture, it can become anything: a spaceship, a farm, or a castle. Without that foundation, it is just colorful chaos. That's how many AI projects unfold: excitement, then confusion.

Almost a decade ago, in one of my former roles, we set out to build a decision intelligence platform for operations. On paper, it looked flawless: strong executive sponsorship, a rapid MVP, and a cross-functional squad ready to deliver. The kick-off had the energy of a toddler's birthday party.

I had just joined the company and sat in the room with C-suite leaders and tech leads. The goals were vague, KPIs were high-level, and the only milestone was "launch MVP in three months." The data maturity, systems readiness, and organizational capacity did not add up, but I stayed quiet, hoping I was wrong. That silence became a very valuable and quite painful career lesson.

Reality landed fast. Discovery was rushed, success metrics were fuzzy, and architecture reviews were superficial. Aspirations were driven top down rather than validated in the field. Soon, it became clear we had no usable data platform, no cloud infrastructure, and no scoped user interface. In short, we were as ready as my toddler showing up at the door with shoes and a jacket, but no trousers.

Progress slid sideways into architecture debates. One squad became three, vendors multiplied, and the Data Privacy Officer became our most frequent collaborator. We were busy rearranging Lego with no baseplate.

The issue was never the model. Our context was not ready.

Eventually, we hit pause and reset. We clarified the goals with measurable business metrics, defined validation methods, and narrowed the scope to a recommendation engine connected directly to frontline workflows. Architecture teams were brought back in, data pipelines were rebuilt, and proper integrations were established. Adoption grew quickly because people trusted the outputs. To keep feedback close and build confidence, we embedded the product lead inside the operational team two days a week. Executives began to see measurable savings, and two years later, the platform was still running, delivering compounding impact.

Context turned it from slideware into a system that worked.

Check your CORE+ prior Takeoff

So what makes some AI projects soar to a smooth landing while others stall on the runway? In my experience, it is rarely the model itself. The difference lies in whether the team runs the equivalent of a pre-flight check with four essentials before takeoff. I call it **CORE+: Clarity, Operations, Readiness,**

and Enablement, plus one more for the age of autonomous agents: **Autonomy Governance.** I never start an AI initiative without it.

Clarity is your flight plan. You need the coordinates of your destination, not just a slogan from the boardroom. What problem are you solving, and how is it handled today? Through endless Excel files, manual workarounds, or half-outsourced fixes? What does it cost, what does it generate, and if fixed, how much more value can be unlocked? Above all, how will success be measured? Imagine planning a holiday to Mallorca but landing in Manchester. Not a bad place, just not where you meant to go.

Operations combine the systems and the people who keep them running. Even the best model is useless if it cannot function in daily reality. Who uses the output and where does it appear in their workflow, in a legacy ERP, a CRM, or yet another window? Do insights trigger action? Are compliance, security, and accountability built into the process? You need people who understand how models behave in the real world, apply the scientific method with discipline, and know when to recalibrate. MLOps practices such as monitoring, retraining, and pipeline management keep systems stable and dashboards reliable once in the air.

Readiness is the runway and the conditions. You may have the most advanced aircraft, but without a clear runway, safe weather, and full visibility, you are not going anywhere. In AI, that means data you can trust - accurate, compliant, and anonymized where needed - systems that connect, and infrastructure that scales without surprises. Integrations must work cleanly, not through fixes held together by duct tape. Models should be explainable, checked for drift and bias, and easy to audit. Skipping these checks is like trying to take off in thick fog without radar.

Enablement prepares crew and passengers. Do frontline teams know how to act on insights? Do managers trust the outputs enough to make decisions? Are teams equipped to govern, challenge, and improve the system? Without this, adoption stalls. The human-AI connection is the most powerful combination for sustained success and can't be approached as an afterthought.

And like aviation, discipline is not only in the check, but in the loop. Every flight teaches something. Experimentation and learning should be your fuel, and teams need both the confidence and space to navigate uncertainty. AI value is real, but as any experienced AI/ML team will tell you, estimating timelines often feels like sailing toward a continent you know exists, just not knowing how far away it is.

With the rise of AI agents, I have added a fifth element: **Autonomy Governance**, which defines when a system can operate without immediate human input, what actions it is allowed to execute, and how oversight is built in. These systems don't "decide"; they process data and act based on encoded logic, learned patterns, or probabilistic inference within boundaries set by humans. The autonomy is functional, not moral. Just as an aircraft autopilot manages flight under the pilot's supervision, AI agents can execute tasks within clearly defined parameters. But it is the pilot who remains accountable for landing safely. Leaders must define those thresholds, when human review is required, when intervention is triggered, and where final accountability stays human. True governance means keeping humans trained, informed, and firmly in command of the loop.

CORE stands, but **CORE+ is what future-proofs it beyond 2025.** It works because context compounds. It turns structure and discipline into real results. Here's how that looks in practice.

Boring Makes Money, Context Compounds

After years of leading automation and AI programs across companies from Nike to an ultra-low-cost airline, the lesson was the same: *boring makes money.*

We learned this the hard way during the RPA wave. Pilots dazzled, but scaling failed. The lesson was not that RPA does not work. It was that context always decides whether it holds. When we got it right and focused on a value stream end-to-end with proper context, the impact followed. In one case, embedding our Technology team with Training revealed process gaps that were not about AI at all. Intelligent process automation solved them faster and cheaper. Within four months, recurring fines disappeared, compliance became automatic, and four FTEs were freed for higher-value work. That win was all about **Operations**, fixing flows across departments, and making the solution run 24/7 in the background.

In another case, we deployed a conversational AI that automated 89% customer inquiries. Response times dropped from minutes to seconds, support costs fell, and satisfaction rose. The real win was **Enablement**, embedding it into customer journeys, compliance, and trust, so it scaled.

In IT support, applying AI to classify, predict, and resolve tickets uncovered the real drivers of demand. The result: faster resolution, fewer delays, and employees who trusted the system. That success hinged on **Readiness**, data pipelines, integrations, and infrastructure that made automation possible.

Across all, credibility came not from a flashy model but from business leaders who owned the outcomes, defined the problems, validated the metrics, and also empowered teams to keep finding the value and embed adoption in daily work. That is **Clarity** in practice: clear goals, measurable results, and leadership that carries the change.

That credibility compounds. Context is your real and only IP - the mix of structure, data, people, and discipline that turns technology into results. It means a deep understanding of the levers of value, the processes that create or waste them, and the systems that connect them all. Once captured and owned, that context becomes leverage.

Even the biggest tech companies cannot copy that. They can sell you the same model as your competitor, but they cannot sell you your ecosystem, your seams, or your operational realities. Context scales differently from tools. Jensen Huang said that future advantage will come from domain expertise, not coding, and he's right. **My addition is this: you won't out-AI Google, but you can out-context anyone.** That's where real leadership is built.

Practical Takeaways

Run the CORE+ check before any AI lift-off.

Start with clarity, not code. The systems, data, and people have to be ready before anything takes off.

+ **Clarity:** Do we know exactly what problem we are solving, how success will be measured, and what value it should create?
+ **Operations:** Is the model integrated where decisions happen, or is it just another dashboard? Do we have the right skills and practices to operate and maintain it?
+ **Readiness:** Is the data complete, compliant, and connected, and can our infrastructure scale safely and cost-effectively?
+ **Enablement:** Are the people who will use it trained, confident, and ready to act on its insights?
+ **Autonomy Governance:** What level of decision-making can safely run without human input, and how is oversight built in? Do we keep human in the loop?

Don't chase headlines, obsess with impact.

Ask: Would we still do this project if it weren't called AI?
If the problem can be solved more simply, that's the right path. Impact shows up in productivity, cost, and trust, not in the press release.

It's never too late to (re)build context

If your first AI attempts fizzled, the issue was likely context. Pause, re-assess, and reset before takeoff. Speed without alignment only compounds waste. Once context is clear, progress compounds.

Personal reflection

I entered the room. It was the final round of interviews for a Technology C-suite role and I was carrying the weight of preparation, ambition, and a healthy amount of nerves. Breathe in, breathe out, I told myself while waiting in front of the meeting room.

It was one of those moments where everything you've worked for feels like it's coming together. My manager had decided to move on. I had been in my role for almost three years, had the right experience, and solid results. It felt like a logical next step. Except for one thing: I was eight months pregnant. Very visibly so.

No one mentioned it during the interviews. I appreciated that.

But outside those formal rooms, with friends and colleagues, I kept getting the same question: "You're interviewing... while pregnant?" At first, I hesitated to say yes. Did it make me overly ambitious? A careerist? A bad mother to be?

Eventually, I understood what was driving me: I've worked so hard to get here. I won't disqualify myself by myself.

That was the moment it clicked. I didn't need to adjust to unspoken rules that were never mine.

I didn't get the role. Someone else did, more experienced, objectively stronger. I would have hired him, too. The timing just wasn't mine.

But here's what followed: I had our baby boy, finished my MBA when he was five months old, and returned to a new leadership role with a bigger scope, business ownership, and revenue accountability.

What's the lesson I want to share? For women, especially moms, there will be phases when our careers slow down. You may get or miss some opportunities. But that is not failure. It's part of the full picture. We need to accept that and stop stepping aside just to avoid making others (and sometimes ourselves) uncomfortable.

Don't disqualify yourself by yourself.

Since stepping into digital transformation and AI leadership, and recently becoming a mother, I have often heard the same hesitation. In meetings, in playgrounds, from colleagues, managers, and parents alike: "I don't know where to start." "I cannot catch up with the pace." Everyone feels it, but it is often women who feel it most.

The truth is, with AI's rapid progress, more than with any previous technology, no one is "there" yet. AI is being shaped every day. That is the unique opportunity we all have right ahead of us. The same way I learned not to step aside in that moment, women must not step aside now in the AI era, because no one is fully ready, and that is the opportunity.

This book is here to show what it really takes to lead and keep going, through doubt, ambition, transition, and change. Not perfect stories, but real ones.

ABOUT THE AUTHOR

VP of Growth × AI, at Automattic, Demet Dagdelen builds AI-powered marketing systems from scratch. With 15+ years at the intersection of ML, causal inference, and marketing, she has created ML platforms, experimentation frameworks, and launched and automated campaigns that generate millions in incremental revenue. After exposing $35M in ad waste through geo-experiments, she rebuilt WordPress.com's growth strategy, achieving 2X industry benchmarks. She writes about incrementality, ML, AI, and growth at incremental.blog.

| 2 |

The Incrementality Revolution: Building Accountable Growth Systems with AI and Causal Inference

When I began this work more than ten years ago, machine learning was still something you had to explain to people in many roles. My first assignment was to build a model that predicted who would convert so we could email them.

The model was flawless. It predicted conversion beautifully. The only problem was, it didn't matter. I split the predicted "likely buyers" into two groups: one received the email, the other didn't. Both converted at the same rate. The model had predicted behavior, but the emails did not influence it. The people we targeted were going to buy anyway.

It highlighted the difference between operational success and strategic success, between doing things and changing things. This is a common pattern in growth work: success measured by how much we do (build models to predict! design campaigns! send emails!), not by what actually changes (true impact on business bottom line).

From that point forward, my focus shifted from prediction to persuasion, from correlation to causation. Over the next decade, that philosophy became the foundation for how we built AI systems, measurement frameworks, and eventually an entire division devoted to sustainable, accountable growth.

This is a story about moving from vanity metrics to accountability, and from isolated ML projects to AI systems that help entire teams make better decisions.

From Prediction to Persuasion

The early email model revealed a bigger truth about marketing's blind spots. Most campaigns reward prediction: who looks promising, who clicked, who converted. But none of that answers the only question that matters—who bought because of us.

We rebuilt around that. Using uplift modeling, an early form of causal AI, we shifted focus from likelihood to influence. The models didn't just predict; they learned who was persuadable.

That change required new infrastructure and, more importantly, a new language. The cultural part mattered as much as the modeling. I stopped talking about model lifts and started talking about user fatigue, forgone future revenue, and the cost of giving discounts to people who would pay full price. That language bridged the gap for peers who lived inside calendars and creative files, not notebooks.

We introduced holdouts by default and replaced static lists with dynamic, daily rescored audiences. The results were unmistakable: fewer emails, lower unsubscribes, and higher incremental revenue.

And we learned something deeper. Good marketing isn't about reach; it's about restraint. Impact scales faster than volume when you know who not to talk to.

The Four Types of Customers in Every Campaign

The first major success came with ML Sales, our email discount campaigns targeting free users. The traditional approach was classic spray-and-pray: email millions of users with the same offer and hope for conversions. The campaigns appeared successful on paper, generating millions in revenue.

But we had no holdouts. No way to measure incremental impact.

I built uplift models to identify four critical user segments:

- Sure Things: Users who convert regardless (giving them discounts loses money)
- Lost Causes: Users who won't convert no matter what. Stop chasing them
- Sleeping Dogs: Users who react negatively to outreach
- Persuadables: The people who buy because of your outreach, the only audience that drives incremental growth, the holy grail of marketing.

Without incrementality and with broad targeting, you're fishing with dynamite. You'll catch something, but you'll destroy the pond. AI-driven targeting lets you fish with precision. It teaches you when to act, when to pause, and when silence is the most strategic move you can make.

Once we switched over from heuristics-based broad targeting to only targeting persuadables via causal modeling & optimizing for incremental purchases, the transformation was dramatic. We were targeting only 20% of people while doubling incremental revenue. Unsubscribes dropped by 70%. Campaign fatigue became manageable through dynamic, AI-driven list updates. Today, these campaigns run in a fully autonomous manner and are responsible for 25% of all new subscriptions.

The Geo Experiment That Changed Company Strategy

Years later, we took these principles to scale. I led a geo experiment to measure whether our multimillion-dollar paid media budget was truly incremental. Inspired by Google's published methods, I built an internal tool to measure lift region by region.

The results were clear. Most of our spending had no measurable effect. The ads looked great in attribution dashboards, but they weren't moving real business outcomes.

We prepared the landing zone for hard truths. If people have no safe next step, they will fight the data. So the CMO expertly paired the results with a plan: shift resources toward organic channels, experimentation, and creative testing while rebuilding paid media with new guardrails.

Then we made the call: pause all paid media.

For two years, we ran no ads. Nothing broke. Revenue held steady. That decision reshaped the company's relationship with marketing metrics and cemented incrementality as the foundation of every growth decision.

Owning the Funnel After Saying "Stop"

When I was asked to lead the relaunch of paid media two years later, I was a data person moving into a marketing seat. I was also the person who had just shut the engine down.

The scary part was not the skepticism. It was the scope. I went from a small team to a cross-functional group that touched creative, landing pages, analytics, data engineering, AI and ML Ops, and channel operations.

I moved from being the person who said "stop" to the person who had to say "go" and prove it could work. I was terrified of breaking the brand, not moving fast enough, moving too fast, or losing the rigor.

We rebuilt paid media from scratch with AI-first foundations:

- Reliable data pipelines that respected privacy and cross-device attribution
- Embedded incrementality, with holdouts and causal testing in every campaign
- AI-driven optimization, continuously learning and adjusting targeting

Within three months, we achieved something unprecedented. Across more than 25 geo experiments on paid media strategy, we found a pocket of incrementality where we saw a 14% lift, compared to typical industry benchmarks of 6–8%. But to scale, we needed the full funnel.

So we expanded to the full lifecycle—connecting acquisition, activation, retention, and upsell through shared data, experiments, and AI systems. Within months, we achieved measurable, incremental lift across the entire funnel, and this infrastructure and system are still in place today, powering our growth.

Making the Right Way the Default

The most fragile thing about an incrementality practice is how much it depends on a few people. When those people leave or get busy, the system drifts back to easy metrics.

To make it stick, we had to make the right way the default.

The goal is to turn hard-won practices into simple defaults:

- Run a campaign, and you get holdouts for free.
- Create an audience, and you see its history and overlap with other emails.
- Launch paid tests, and you're prompted to attach the right experimental design.
- Generate copy, and AI enforces brand voice and tone guardrails automatically, protecting trust while speeding up creative iteration.

When good hygiene is easy, it compounds. Over time, discipline becomes culture.

Scaling Impact: Building AI-Powered Growth Infrastructure

Today, I lead Growth Infrastructure, a division that builds the AI systems and data foundations for responsible growth.

We are building the marketing automation systems that power over a billion customer communications a month. It consolidates what used to be dozens of disconnected tools into one platform where every campaign is measurable, every audience is dynamic, and every action ties back to incremental impact.

- Automatic holdouts ensure honest measurement.
- AI-powered audience scoring adapts daily to behavioral signals.
- Campaign taxonomies create consistency across brands and products.
- Unified analytics focus on causal impact, not vanity metrics.
- AI-assisted creative testing scales learning without breaking tone or trust.

The harder part was cultural, not technical. I had to translate causal inference into plain business language. For finance, it meant incremental returns. For marketing, brand trust. For executives, sustainable growth. I learned that change happens when rigor meets relevance.

AI is now amplifying that rigor. It's helping us build growth systems that learn, test, and optimize autonomously while keeping human judgment at the center.

Communication, Trust, and the Long Game

The technical pieces are teachable. The human ones take longer.

Translate for the real job. When I was speaking into the void, I was talking about uplift, ATEs, and statistical power. My peers were thinking about creative fatigue, customer promises, and predictable revenue. I switched to talking about list health, fatigue, and long-term value. The models didn't get simpler. The story did.

Do not make anyone the villain. The goal isn't to prove someone wrong; it's to create a system that makes it easy to be right. People were doing the best they could with the tools they had. Now we have better ones.

Create visible wins that matter. Small, measurable victories build trust faster than big claims. A holdout that shows lower unsubscribes and higher cash per user is more powerful than a thousand-word slide deck.

Prepare the next landing zone. When results disrupt expectations, have a safe, credible path forward. No one follows data into a void.

This is the long game. **Culture shifts when accountability feels like empowerment, not inspection.**

Closing Thought

Incrementality isn't a purist stance. It's how you focus on the only metric that matters: did something change because of you.

When you build around that question, creative gets sharper, targeting gets kinder, and spend gets calmer. You stop chasing movement and start designing impact.

AI and automation extend that principle. We can build systems that reason, test, and adapt on their own—systems that don't just automate marketing, but understand impact. The future of growth isn't about speed for its own sake. It's about truth at scale.

Personal reflection

The Day a "Win" Felt Wrong

Ten years ago, I built a model that perfectly predicted conversions. The company celebrated. But when I tested it, I realized it didn't change anything. That was the day I stopped measuring success by prediction and started measuring it by causation.

Since then, every project I've led - uplift modeling, geo experiments, AI automation, and global marketing systems - has followed the same rule: prediction is cheap; change is rare and valuable.

A few years later, the geo experiments proved that our multimillion-dollar paid media program wasn't driving incremental growth, so we paused it entirely.

When I was later asked to lead the relaunch of paid media, the very program I had once shut down, it felt full circle. The person who had stopped the ads was now responsible for reimagining how they could work.

I wasn't afraid of moving too fast. I was afraid of not moving fast enough to embed rigor before scale. I learned that AI isn't about replacing human judgment; it's about scaling it.

If there's a thread through all of it, it's this: **rigor fuels creativity. When you measure what truly matters and build guardrails that optimize for them, people make braver decisions, move faster, and build systems that outlast them.**

ABOUT THE AUTHOR

As Head of Cloud & AI, Klaudia Czarnecka-Kowcun leads the strategy, development, and adoption of cloud and artificial intelligence solutions at Software Mind.

Her mission is to accelerate digital transformation, enhance operational efficiency, and enable data-driven innovation across the business. She manages cross-functional teams and partners with senior stakeholders to ensure technology investments drive measurable business outcomes.

| 3 |

MCP Servers: The Invisible Backbone of AI-Native Enterprises

The last few years have been a festival of enthusiasm surrounding Artificial Intelligence. Everyone is "pro-AI," but we, the leaders responsible for enterprise-scale deployments, know that there is a vast, expensive gulf between a pioneer demo and a production rollout at corporate scale.

We call this the "last mile of AI" problem. The models are intelligent, but their secure, scalable, and compliant connection to 50 different internal systems (our company's historical DNA) is an enormous engineering and legal challenge.

This is where Model Context Protocol (MCP) Servers come in. They cease to be a mere technical detail and become the critical, yet often invisible, backbone that allows large enterprises to truly scale their AI integration. Our goal: to move AI away from being a fashionable overlay and embed it as a native element of business processes.

In this article, we will examine this technological breakthrough that is moving us from the era of talking chatbots to AI Agents that can securely act, make decisions, and generate revenue.

The Challenge: Why AI Crashes Into the Corporate Wall

Architectural Chaos and the Problem of "Internal Inconsistency"

The biggest enemy of scalability in a large corporation is the lack of an integration standard.

Most corporations possess hundreds of systems, each with its own API and communication rules. Before the MCP era, there was no overall, standardized way for AI to communicate with these systems.

The result was architectural chaos within the organization:

+ Duplication and Variation: Team A, building an AI Agent for finance, had to write an integration to a core database in their preferred language and unique style. Team B, building an Agent for logistics that needed access to the exact same database, wrote the integration again, in a different language and with different error-handling logic. The result was two different, costly, and potentially inconsistently operating integrations for the same corporate resource.

- Costly Technical Debt: Each of these custom integrations became technical debt at light speed. It required separate maintenance, documentation, and testing every time the AI model or the underlying API was updated.

I recall an instance early in my career, well before the MCP standard emerged, where a seemingly minor update to a legacy accounting API completely crashed our nascent AI-powered recommendation engine. Why? Because the two teams responsible for the integration had used different libraries and documented the failure modes differently. We wasted three weeks just resolving a conflict between two internal versions of the 'same' integration. It was a costly, frustrating demonstration that complexity is a tax on innovation. That moment solidified my belief that we needed to stop solving problems on a case-by-case basis and mandate a unified communication language.

Agent Operational Blindness and Errors That Cost Money

An AI Agent that lacks access to real-time data and the ability to act is merely a highly articulate model that can summarize historical documents. Such an agent is not worth the investment.

The consequences of lacking up-to-date context are simple and expensive:

- Lack of Precision (Hallucinations): In an enterprise environment, a hallucination is not a funny mistake. It is an error on an invoice, an incorrect diagnosis, or a wrongly submitted request. This erodes customer trust and costs the company reputation.
- Agent Uselessness: An Agent that can write a perfect email to a client, but cannot autonomously create a new account for them in the system, remains only an expensive assistant that generates work instead of automating it.

Until now, the attempt to connect AI to executive systems (e.g., accounting systems) has been too complicated and uncertain.

Threat to Risk and Compliance

The biggest hurdle for scalable AI is Security and Corporate Governance.

In the traditional approach, for an AI Agent to function, it often received overly broad permissions, operating on an "all or nothing" basis. Such Agent's "omniscience" constitutes a huge risk.

Lack of Granular Control: How do we ensure that the HR assistant doesn't accidentally gain access to the Management Board's financial data?

Manipulation Risk: How do we prevent a maliciously constructed query (the so-called prompt injection) from forcing the Agent to perform an unauthorized transaction?

Consequently, Compliance and Risk Management departments rightfully block projects. And this is where the MCP Server emerges as the single, trusted control point that enables action while ensuring full control and compliance with regulations.

The Solution, Impact & Reflection - MCP: Value, Scale, and Audit

The MCP Architecture: Unification and a Universal Port for Business Value

The Model Context Protocol (MCP) is an open standard that should be understood as a universal communication interface for all our corporate knowledge and tools. Its key value is that it enforces an internal integration standard across the entire organization.

How this translates to business and architecture:

| 1 MCP Server as a Functionality Slice: The MCP Server acts as an adapter, which exposes only a strictly defined set of business functionalities, for example, only: "Check product availability" or "Approve vacation request". This unifies the way all internal teams use the same resource, eliminating the internal chaos described earlier.

|2 One Protocol – Any Model (Decoupling): This is the key to scalability and architectural flexibility. An already built, secure MCP Server for our financial system will work with every AI model on the market, the one we use today, and the one that will emerge next year. This is the end of vendor lock-in at the integration layer.

|3 Intelligent Action (Agent Framework): The AI model doesn't have to guess how to act. It receives a list of its capabilities and tools from the MCP Server in a clear, standardized language, allowing it to autonomously take the next steps and actually execute complex tasks.

In this way, MCP Servers break down silos, creating a Unified AI Ecosystem that doesn't ask where the data is from, but "what action can the model perform with it?"

Case Study: Atlassian Rovo: Secure Knowledge Access Control

A perfect, real-world example of moving from "demo" to "production" is the architecture behind Atlassian Rovo.

- Business Challenge: An engineer asks AI for a project status. How can context be delivered from Jira and Confluence (where the knowledge resides) while ensuring the model only sees the documents and tasks to which the specific employee has permission?

- MCP Servers Solution: Atlassian built a Remote MCP Server that acts as a gatekeeper of access and translator of corporate knowledge.
  - Permissions and Identity Filter: The MCP Server is tightly integrated with the company's Identity and Access Management (IAM) system. This means the MCP Server respects and enforces existing corporate permissions. If a user only has access to 5 out of 50 projects, their AI Agent will see context only from those 5 projects. The MCP Server is the permissions police in the AI world.
  - Compliance and Authorization: Everything is embedded within a full OAuth mechanism, with auditable logs. The MCP Server is a trusted entry point that ensures every action taken by Agents complies with company policy and regulations.

From a Director of Cloud & AI perspective, this is a triumph. Only this level of granular security and auditability can unlock investment in full-scale AI agent deployment.

Competitive Advantage: Creating a Unified AI Ecosystem

Deploying MCP is not just about improving integration; it is a fundamental shift in how we think about technology. By focusing on this protocol, we are creating a Unified AI Ecosystem.

In this new environment:

- The AI Agent is no longer a separate, isolated application; it becomes an executive unit plugged into a centralized corporate service catalog.
- The IT department no longer writes custom plugins; it creates a repository of trusted MCP Servers and manages access to them, adhering to the principle of an AI Service Catalog.

Specific Market Advantage:

|1 Speed to Value: We can scale across the entire organization. When the business identifies a new automation need, we don't wait for costly new integration; we expose the existing MCP Servers. The AI Agent is ready to work immediately, understanding the context.

|2 Controlled Innovation: Instead of building one expensive, monolithic model, we can create a network of specialized, lower-cost Agents, each utilizing MCP to focus only on its narrow specialization. This is the recipe for optimizing inference costs.

|3 Foundation of Trust (Compliance by Design): By enforcing security by design at the protocol level (Audit, Access Control), AI gains the trust required by the Management Board, Compliance, and Customers. We are able to prove that our AI operates responsibly and lawfully.

Personal Reflection as a Leader: Building the Foundations

AI is a marathon, not a sprint. After years of watching innovations fail under the weight of architectural chaos and risk, I see a fundamental change in MCP. What I appreciate most about this revolution is that the infrastructure the foundation that we, the people in Cloud & AI, build is finally taking center stage.

I've spent my career building cloud foundations, and the most critical lesson I learned didn't come from a server room; it came from watching my grandmother maintain her century-old family home. She wasn't focused on the paint color or the fancy new gadgets; she was obsessed with the foundation, the drainage, and the roof. She'd say, "Klaudia, you can't build a bright future on rotten beams."

Professionally, this translates directly to my approach to AI. I've always prioritized the unsexy work: the governance, the security protocols, the solid data pipelines. When a project is shiny and fast, I'm the one asking, "What's the drainage plan?"

MCP Servers embody this grounded, foundational thinking. They are the "drainage and foundation" for AI: invisible, but essential for protecting the entire corporate structure. This focus on building something that lasts, that is robust enough to handle the storm is what guides my decisions as a leader in this high-speed, hype-driven industry. We must build for trust and longevity, not just for the next quarterly demo.

Prawdziwa transformacja (True transformation) is not about having the most expensive AI model, but about the ability to securely and scalably connect it to enterprise resources.

So, are we ready to move from the testing phase to the phase of scaling our AI Agents? The decision is ours. As leaders, we must stop focusing on *what* AI can do, and start building the infrastructure that will actually allow AI to operate and generate value.

ABOUT THE AUTHOR

Katia is a startup expert and the founder of Block-333, a boutique consultancy. She currently serves as an Execution Partner for the Emerging Tech Innovation Lab at 1871 in Chicago, where she focuses on building relationships with key investors and accelerators. Katia actively mentors early-stage AI and Web3 startups across the US and EMEA, guiding founders through go-to-market strategies and fundraising. She holds an MBA from the Kellogg School of Management.

Katia Kobylinski, MBA

| 4 |

Building the AI-First Accelerator: A New Blueprint for Founder Success

AI appears to be one of the fastest adopted new technologies of all time [4]. AI enterprise value is already worth about $13.1 trillion USD [5], and investments in AI now account for a substantial and rapidly growing share of all venture capital deals. With these mind-blowing numbers in mind, it is impossible to assume that the long-established accelerator playbook for how startups are founded, funded, and exited will remain untouched. In fact, it is rapidly evolving right in front of our eyes.

The foundation of every successful startup ecosystem—the accelerator model—is facing an existential inflection point.

While accelerators have historically served diverse verticals like health tech, consumer applications, and fintech, the traditional blueprint was overwhelmingly designed and optimized for the Software-as-a-Service (SaaS) model. This SaaS-first framework is, however, ill-equipped to serve the new wave of AI-native ventures. These startups operate with a completely different logic and context, rooted not just in code, but in unique data access, delivering instantaneous user value, and fundamentally transforming customer workflows.

I do not purport to know everything about the long-term impact of AI on startup accelerator success. Those who claim they can name all facets of this disruption probably lack imagination. Given the rapid pace of AI adoption across the entire tech stack, it is hardly possible to see beyond a one-to-two-year horizon. Instead, I intend to provide elements of a blueprint for innovation hubs and startup accelerators, drawing on my experience as an Execution Partner for the 1871 Emerging Tech Innovation Summit in Chicago, based on what we know now and what we can reasonably expect in the near future. This is a guide for the people who build ecosystems, showing how to design programs that turn nascent AI visions into defensible, high-growth ventures.

One thing is clear - we must move beyond syllabi that treat AI as a mere feature. **The AI-First Accelerator Model** outlined here is a direct response to this urgent need, addressing the unique challenges of the data lifecycle, technical talent acquisition, ethical AI deployment, and achieving algorithmic defensibility—the ultimate moat for the modern startup.

The 1871 Great Chicago Fire: From Disruption to Innovation

I spent eight years of my life in the great city of Chicago, the home of 1871, a collective of trailblazing founders, visionary leaders, resilient innovators, and steadfast supporters in tech. The name 1871 is derived from the year of the Great Chicago Fire. A legend has it that a cow of a certain Mrs. O'Leary was to blame. The cow allegedly kicked over a kerosene lantern, which then ignited the hay and the barn, thus starting a massive conflagration that would destroy much of the city. To be very clear, at 1871, we do not celebrate the fire itself. We celebrate the massive wave of innovation that flooded the city in the years to come. The age of AI represents yet another "industrial revolution" that is redefining the rules of the game.

The Evolution of the Traditional Accelerator Playbook

For decades, the accelerator's infrastructure was largely built on the **SaaS paradigm**, prioritizing linear growth loops and feature iteration. This framework is obsolete for AI-native companies, as the fundamental logic has reversed. The legacy blueprint cannot fully accommodate the non-linear compute expenses, the product hazard of model reliability, and the necessary pivot from code IP to data and algorithmic defensibility. Modern AI-native startups ultimately face unique operating logic, making the previous accelerator model obsolete:

SaaS Focus	AI-Native Reality
PMF as Feature Iteration	Product-Market-Fit (PMF henceforth) depends on the AI Model working reliably. If the AI gives weird or biased answers ("hallucinates"), no amount of tweaking the buttons and colors will fix the core product failure.
Simple Scalability	AI companies face high, unpredictable Running Costs. A simple $10 trial model can jump to $10,000 when scaled up, instantly wiping out all profit margins.
The Moat: Code as IP	The real defense is the Unique Data and the automated process that constantly makes the AI smarter. Legal advice must focus on protecting this data asset, not just the code itself.
Static Legal Compliance	Dynamic Regulatory Risk. The rules for AI are constantly changing. Founders must build evolving compliance directly into their core strategy for every market they enter, as old legal playbooks are useless.
Linear Team Scaling	Accessibility of AI tools means founders can achieve substantial scale with smaller teams. What a team of 20 generalists would achieve in the past can now be done by 5 highly leveraged founders, fundamentally changing hiring and team management.

What is Staying: The Enduring Fundamentals

With so many fundamentals transforming, it would be easy to succumb to either indecisiveness regarding the next step or pressure to revamp absolutely everything. At times of enormous uncertainty and change, when predicting even a near future feels like a Herculean effort, it is often more helpful to ask - what is likely to remain the same? - and perhaps start from there.

In my conversations with AI-native startup founders on both sides of the Atlantic, I found that many things they expect from a leading accelerator program are often (almost) timeless. Indeed, certain foundational elements of a successful accelerator program remain the same, albeit they will require updated context and content:

- **Company Building Basics:** Fundamental principles like understanding cap tables, incorporating, and basic financial hygiene are timeless and still necessary for any high-growth venture, including in emerging tech.
- **Human-Centric B2B Sales Strategy:** While AI can optimize lead generation and pre-qualify customers, complex B2B sales still rely on human skills: building trust, navigating internal politics, customizing deals, and negotiating terms.
- **Mentorship:** A strong mentor network remains key, but its focus has shifted. As AI handles information-gathering, mentors' unique value lies in providing

personal connections, insider knowledge, and lived experience that cannot be automated.

- **Investor Relations:** Despite VCs using AI to scan millions of data points for leads, closing deals and negotiating terms still rely entirely on human interaction, trust, and the founder's personal reputation and recommendations.
- **Networking and Peer Support:** The core value of connecting founders with peers facing similar existential struggles (e.g., how to hire and retain experienced AI/ML talent) remains paramount. While some challenges might be new, the need for connectedness is here to stay.

In my work with an Estonian start-up, an AI-native early-stage startup specializing in the gamification of HR training, I found precisely that. Although AI was absolutely core to the start-up's idea and, as such, embedded in business strategy, it became clear that what we needed the most at this stage of growth was a solid and time-tested B2B go-to-market strategy, coupled with access to the right resources and mentors to help facilitate the next step - expansion to the US market.

While the pillars that I highlighted above will certainly need to evolve together with the changing context and new developments brought about by AI, the story shows that tapping into the fundamentals is unlikely to get old, and every accelerator should be absolutely making sure to get the timeless foundation right.

What is Evolving: The New Fundamentals

The tension between the obsolete SaaS playbook and the enduring human needs of startup founders, however, also necessitates a rewrite of the accelerator curriculum. The new AI-First Accelerator Model must equip founders not just with basic business skills, but also with a new operational calculus for managing data, processing power, and algorithmic risk.

The starting point is acknowledging the AI shift. This commitment mandates updating the Enduring Fundamentals to the new reality. Following this groundwork, the program should develop the new, essential curriculum, focusing on the pillars explored in this section.

1. Algorithmic PMF and Model Reliability

The traditional accelerator taught PMF through rapid feature iteration. For AI-native ventures, this is fundamentally flawed. PMF is now **Algorithmic PMF**: the product fails if the underlying model is unreliable, biased, or inaccurate. The new curriculum must train founders to focus on:

- **Defining Reliability as a Feature**: Model quality (avoiding hallucinations, maintaining low variance) is the core product feature that builds customer trust.
- **Product Quality Assurance**: Implementing simple practices to continually monitor models in production. This is essential to prevent performance degradation

(model drift), which directly breaks customer experience.

+ **Minimum Viable Dataset (MVD)**: Shifting from an MVP to finding the smallest, most unique dataset required to prove the model can solve the customer's problem effectively.

2. The New Unit Economics: Processing Power and Value-Based Pricing

In the SaaS world, marginal costs trended toward zero. AI has inverted this; every API [6] call and GPU [7] cycle generates a real, measurable cost. The accelerator must now focus on **Compute Economics**:

+ **Non-Linear Cost Modeling**: Training founders to accurately forecast their "compute burn rate." A product that is profitable in a pilot may bankrupt the company at scale if the computational cost is not tightly managed.

+ **Value-Based Pricing**: Moving away from seat licenses. If an AI agent performs the job of two human analysts, the product must be priced on the value delivered (e.g., per report, per task completed) rather than per user.

3. AI-Native Organizational Design and High-Leverage Teams

The old playbook focused on scaling headcount linearly; the new focus is on maximizing the leverage of a small, highly specialized team through AI tools. The new focus for founders is:

- **Specialist Talent Strategy**: Shifting hiring focus from generalist engineers to the hyper-specific challenge of attracting and retaining AI/ML and Data Science talent, which offers disproportionate product leverage.
- **AI-Augmented Workflows**: Training teams to be "AI-first" in their daily operations, leveraging LLMs for everything from customer support to writing internal documentation, allowing smaller teams to achieve massive output.

4. Data Strategy as Algorithmic Defensibility

The ultimate moat for an AI startup is its Algorithmic Defensibility, achieved when proprietary customer data continuously feeds back into and improves the core model, creating a widening performance gap. The accelerator must shift its IP focus to:

- **Data Rights as IP:** Securing formal data rights and ensuring the legal lineage of training data, treating proprietary data as the most valuable intellectual property (IP).

- **The Data Feedback Loop:** Helping founders design the product experience specifically to collect the most valuable, unique data points, which strengthens the model's performance moat.
- **Proprietary vs. Commoditized Data:** Teaching founders to distinguish between easily accessible data and truly proprietary data, and prioritizing the latter for competitive advantage.

5. Ethical and Regulatory Strategy as a Core Moat

In the age of emerging AI, compliance is no longer a legal afterthought; it is a necessity for enterprise adoption. Treating legal and regulatory risk as an external factor can be lethal. The evolved curriculum must embed this discipline as a core business strategy because:

- **Compliance is Product Strategy:** Regulatory and bias review must be integrated into the product development lifecycle from day one. This is a core product function because AI is still an emerging tech space, and its legal framework changes by the day.
- **Dynamic Legal Landscape:** Founders must build evolving compliance directly into their core strategy for every market they enter, as static legal playbooks are useless given the constantly changing global rules.

- **Ethical Review as Trust:** Demonstrating a commitment to ethical AI and bias mitigation is increasingly a non-negotiable requirement for closing large enterprise sales deals, making it a competitive advantage.

Tactical Takeaways for Tomorrow

For leaders building the next generation of startup ecosystems, immediate action should center on integrating timeless human capital with the new AI calculus:

- **Redefine Mentorship to Focus on Scarcity:** Shift your mentor network's priority from general business advice to providing proprietary context and insider network access. When general information is free (via AI), the unique value of a human mentor is their rolodex and their ability to vet the origin (lineage) of a founder's core training data—the startup's true IP.
- **Re-engineer Your Unit Economics Curriculum:** Immediately replace "simple scalability" modules with workshops on Non-Linear Cost Modeling. Teach founders to price their product based on the value delivered (human job displaced) rather than simple subscription seats, ensuring the inevitable, high non-linear computational cost is covered from day one.
- **Establish Trust as a Competitive Moat:** Utilize your cohort's shared experience by setting up Peer-to-

Peer Compliance Sprints. This structural change dynamically embeds ethical and regulatory strategy into the core business model, transforming risk from a liability into a competitive moat that proactively unlocks large enterprise sales and guarantees alignment with the rapidly evolving legal landscape.

Next Steps into the Unknown

The Great Chicago Fire serves as a powerful reminder that massive disruption is invariably followed by unprecedented innovation. Today, the surge of AI adoption is dismantling the accelerator playbook, compelling ecosystem builders to actively lead the rebuild. The choice is clear—we must move beyond the predictable, feature-driven world of SaaS.

The new reality demands a strategic pivot, prioritizing Algorithmic PMF, mastering non-linear Compute Economics, and embedding Ethical and Data Strategy as core business functions. The human elements—trust, mentorship, and peer support—remain timeless, but their context is irrevocably changed. For innovation hubs across the globe, the time for incremental updates is over. By embracing this AI-First Accelerator Model and applying this new blueprint, we ensure we teach founders how to build the defensible, high-leverage ventures that will define the next industrial revolution.

Personal Reflection: The Timeless Value of an MBA

The decision to pursue an MBA at the Kellogg School of Management had been on my mind for years, a persistent ambition balanced by significant doubt. The timing always felt terrifying. Why commit to a second graduate degree—a huge, expensive leap that meant incurring significant debt—when AI was starting to make formal education increasingly obsolete? The conventional wisdom suggested I should be coding, building, and learning from market failure, not sitting in a classroom in Evanston (United States). Yet, I knew I would regret it if I didn't take the chance. My ultimate decision wasn't driven by guaranteed financial gain, but by a deeper trust in the long-term, multifaceted ROI of the Kellogg experience. Looking back, this MBA has been one of the best professional decisions I have made thus far, precisely because it equipped me to lead in this new, unpredictable reality.

The enduring value of an MBA lies not in the diploma itself but in the time spent solidifying the timeless foundations of doing business, broadening horizons in numerous and nascent fields, learning to navigate the disruption, and honing leadership skills through working with real businesses around the world.

Ultimately, Kellogg equipped me with a critical dual perspective. On one hand, the formal education in finance, venture capital, and business strategy drilled in the timeless fundamentals: how to model true unit economics, structure cap tables, and be on the lookout for non-market factors. On the other hand, my experiential curriculum—particularly my independent research on the enterprise adoption of emerging decentralized technology and social impact projects I worked on with my peers across Latin America—broadened my horizons in ways I could not have imagined.

But the real, irreplaceable value was the network. As I argue in my main essay, when information becomes commoditized by AI, the unique contribution of a mentor is insider knowledge and personal connections. Kellogg delivered this density of human capital: a ready-made ecosystem spanning angels, VCs, visionary entrepreneurs and professionals from across industries, as well as career coaches and faculty. It isn't about what I know, but who I can ask—and more importantly, who I can build trust with. This community is my true ROI.

The MBA surely didn't give me the answers to the AI revolution, but it did teach me that while technology may change the game every eighteen months, the principles of value creation and the power of human trust remain constant.

PART II: LEADERSHIP SYSTEMS

How real transformation happens inside organizations that make AI work.

ABOUT THE AUTHOR

Emma is the CEO and co-founder of Spriggun, a digital transformation and tech advisory firm. Previously, she led the Global Data Privacy function at a FTSE 100 company, with responsibility for legal and operational privacy, cyber legal, and data governance. Emma has held senior roles across tech, workforce solutions, and banking, with a consistent focus on the intersection of law, technology, and governance. Before her legal career, she worked in EU and UK policy, and continues to engage with international policy in the digital and data domains.

Emma Di Iorio

| 5 |

Unlocking Value and Enabling Trust: Holistic Data Strategy as an Enabler of Responsible AI and Digital Transformation

Unlocking value and enabling trust is the concept that organisational (and societal) value and competitive advantage can be achieved while enabling trust. Ultimately, technological developments must benefit humans, with humans, not be *done to* humans. Contrary to mainstream thinking, your approach to regulatory compliance can be a competitive advantage, rather than a burden. The explosive growth, especially of generative

AI since 2023, opens up significant opportunities beyond the typical lenses of legal, risk, and compliance. It is both desirable and possible to take a holistic and multifunctional approach to data and tech strategy, as the foundation for ensuring both effective business outcomes *and* a responsible approach to AI and developing technologies.

Part I: Foundations

Technology, Technology, Technology!

Let us begin with the elephant in the room: all companies are data, and tech, companies; and those that do not adapt to this are unlikely to thrive. If your organisation is not utilising data and AI effectively, your competitors likely are (though in 2025, potentially with no ROI, so here is your opportunity). Flip this to a more positive outlook: even if your organisation is not currently data-focused or tech-first, there is time. Those at the front are only about six months ahead, and those behind are only about a year behind, given how quickly data, AI, and tech are moving.

KYD (& KYAI) - Go slow to go fast

Know your data (KYD): how much do you have; how complete and accurate is it; where it is kept and how it is protected - can this data achieve the goals you want to achieve, in its current form? If not, is your leadership aware that work must be done to get data-ready, how long this will take, and what it will cost (including if new data must be acquired)? I have been told across sectors, and businesses, that KYD is an unnecessary step in the way of reaching a solution quickly, only for the solution not to meet the intended objectives due to data that isn't fit for purpose. I cannot stress how important KYD is, and the added utility for future use cases if done well. To get the most value from data and tech solutions, build foundations for developing business needs, considering medium-long-term goals, rather than focusing solely on short-termist ROI.

If possible, get to a single source of truth for the data you hold, including master data and metadata. You may already have a data inventory/mapping/retention schedule; useful building blocks for data tagging and classification. Otherwise, start data mapping today. Also, map the (likely existing) shadow AI [8] in your organisation (KYAI) and in-scope data, as far as possible. If there is a disconnect between the data in hand and leadership expectations, it's a good idea to flag this as soon as possible.

More is not always more

More data is useful if you can make a positive change by utilising it quickly; tangibly improve products; add value for (current or future) product users; and if it does not become obsolete so quickly to make it of limited use. More data is not useful in and of itself, if records (e.g. consumer contact details) don't translate into improving your end-user/consumer experience or better products; posing an increased risk and cyber attack area. Of course, many AI/ML solutions need significant data sets, but it's still important to collect what you need (only) - if you need five data fields, don't collect fifteen. Consider how data might be utilised as part of a solution to a business problem; to better serve your customers, consumers, clients, and partners. In deciding whether to build or buy AI solutions, do what you do best - vanilla use cases don't likely need building, but buy and adapt. Traditionally, non-tech companies may not see a benefit from a pivot to create their own model. Indeed, beware of shiny objects without a specific application to your organisational needs. Consider what data you already have, what you can do with it, and whether additional data adds additional marginal value to your offering.

Data quality across the data lifecycle

If you already KYD, do you know where each data set came from, and what you can do with the data (including personal and commercially sensitive data and IP rights)? Consider the true blockers to achieving your business goals and associated risks. To move quickly, don't boil the ocean; rather, use KYD and ideation to align your highest business priorities and risks of not acting. How can you solve for these, especially in areas that are public/consumer/customer-facing?

It is a great idea to review your data catalogue; does the data and tagging make sense? Do you have an effective metadata management platform, data lineage, and data quality monitoring tools? If not, take a strong look at these.

Correcting inaccurate or incomplete data is not exciting (and is often time-consuming and costly), but doing it well means you're building future solutions - including those you may not yet realise you need or want - on strong foundations. Legacy tech poses additional challenges, along with rationalising and consolidating existing apps and tools.

To get started, it may not be a blocker to continue as is - for low-risk use cases - utilising AI solutions to rationalise unstructured data. However, building on quicksand is not a viable long-term organisational solution. Eat the KYD, KYAI, and data quality elephant, one bite at a time: incremental change is better than no change.

Part II: Holistic Data Strategy

Effective holistic data strategy, and its implementation, hangs on:

Top Down Data Governance

Executive sponsorship and support - including accountability sitting with a member of the C-suite - is crucial. To achieve success, and to enable leadership to choose the best investment priorities, give leaders sufficient data and technical understanding to enable true buy-in and alignment - workshopping can help.

Top-down data governance needs a multifunctional approach, including:

- Centralised data governance board, responsible for data strategy - including clear roles and responsibilities;
- Governance policies and processes, forming a comprehensive framework for data management and usage; and
- Aligning and cascading shared terminology throughout the organisation.

A centralised governance model ensures consistent definitions and data quality, allowing quicker market analysis and product launches. Early consideration and clarification of roles can reduce duplication of work and prevent costly errors. To go from solely risk-thinking to innovation, data risk management must be embedded in the context of increasing regulatory scrutiny in the data and tech space.

Building Data Into Business Strategy

Establish your enterprise data strategy so it is a core part of your corporate strategy and growth. This is an organisation-wide programme, not an IT project (or CIO/CTO/CDAO's sole responsibility). While democratisation and decentralisation of data usage add value in some circumstances, consider a hub and spoke approach, with top-down data governance, enabling a data ownership framework, led by a single function (e.g., under CDAO). Utilise multifunctional squads to deliver value quickly. Domain experts are key to solving the specific business problems at stake, rather than looking at data science in a silo. Indeed, if you're a lawyer working across data, tech, AI, and digital transformation, your CDO, CDAO, and CISO are some of your most important relationships to foster. Lastly, think global, think local: on-the-ground business knowledge is especially important when it comes to interpreting data from other countries. For multinationals, understanding local business logic and local legislation should be woven in.

Enhancing organisational data maturity is key to succeeding, without which business-critical decisions are likely to be made on data that is out of date, incomplete, inaccurate, or all three.

Establish business ownership and accountability for data quality within the data ownership framework. In a legal, risk, and regulatory context, a product legal approach can help with taking an holistic approach; unlocking data and enabling trust. Lastly, bring people with you! A cultural shift is needed, likely requiring change management to embed new ways of working throughout the organisation. This goes significantly beyond issuing communications, with all staff training (basic and enhanced, depending on the data-centricity of their role) key.

Straddling law, policy & tech expertise - Accountable AI is not an extra

There is no AI without data - this is sometimes forgotten! Privacy, security, responsibility, and accountability must be baked in: built on a sound understanding of the data and tech in scope; and in the context of ever more entwined privacy, data, AI, and cybersecurity legislation. The introduction of both the EU AI Act [9] and NIS2 [10] within the EU, and similar legislation across APAC, LATAM, the US, and Africa, increases the need for a holistic approach.

So, what do you need to do to achieve good privacy, security and accountability within AI, and digital transformation? Firstly, understand the patchwork of global legislation, understand the tech and data in scope, and understand how these fit together with your organisational needs. That minimum legal requirements must be met is a no-brainer, but this is not a compliance exercise. In addition to your usual work: on legal basis, data minimisation (and privacy-AI tension), transparency, data retention, authentication, encryption, and security monitoring; do you know your algorithm(s), expected outputs, and is effective edge-case testing in place? [11]

In the advent of AI, the regulatory stakes are higher, with previously non-personal data potentially reidentifiable due to the high number of records and data points, and non-sensitive data potentially used to predict or infer sensitive info. This brings significantly more data within global privacy regimes and a cyber regulatory view. With data privacy legislation -

including through enforcement from data protection regulators - shaping AI development, the privacy foundations you already have in place are good foundations on which to build broader AI risk (and reward) reviews. Consider a one-stop shop: including ESG, competition/antitrust, consumer protection, and online harm requirements; streamlining your review process; gaining a truly holistic view of the risks and rewards; and reducing repetitive compliance processes, common in multinationals.

While none of the above gives a straightforward ROI figure, by doing a great job in this area, you are likely to reduce the risk of litigation; increase trust (and potential brand loyalty) with those who use your products or services; and open access to markets with more stringent regulatory regimes. Ongoing tracking of regulatory and technological developments and considering synergies between legislative regimes, can enable faster regulatory and technological adaption. Lastly, human experience should be improved by AI - there may not (yet) be legislation in place to prevent you from doing something, but accountable and responsible AI remains key.

Part III: Practical takeaways

Start thinking like a data and tech company

Set company-specific rules for data usage; build a multifunctional data-focused team; and engage your C-suite lead. Ensure each use case has a clear, measurable (and longer-term) ROI - don't jump into AI pilots without business goal alignment and rollout plan.

Data Governance is sexy

Embedding data governance can enable better insights and quicker decision-making, leading to faster and more accurate analytics than competitors:

- KYD & KYAI is an ongoing programme - Make data accessible and trustworthy across the business.
- Understand the impact of your algorithms and data use, to prevent harm, and faster integrate new systems, products, and services.
- Begin the cultural change, including your data principles in company-wide training, and embeddedness beyond data literacy to data fluency.

Use holistic legal, policy, and tech expertise as a competitive advantage

A strong and deep understanding across legal and regulatory, technology, and data enables a transformed approach to AI and digital transformation, taking data from a risk to a strategic asset:

- Quicker time to market and innovation readiness, through a holistic understanding.

- Improving customer trust, possible with strong compliance and transparency as a differentiator, including brilliant boring compliance basics.

Personal reflection: Squiggly is good.

For the past two decades, I've been at the crossroads of policy, law, and technology, navigating shifting landscapes across multiple sectors. This chapter is born from that journey — told through the lens of a data and technology lawyer, yet stretching far beyond into the realms of geopolitics, international regulation, emerging technologies, and the unfolding world of AI. Here, law meets strategy, privacy meets innovation, and governance meets global change. What follows reflects not only years of practice but also conversations from conference stages where I've spoken on AI, regulation, and the life cycle of data — a blend of experience, insight, and a sense of where the future might take us.

I began my career in EU and international policy. I relished the intellectual challenge of novel policy problems, always with a tech thread running through. However, having thought I could do good by working in policy (in the criminal justice and higher education spaces mainly), it was not for me, and I moved into law for my second career. My defining moment was realising I could change careers, and it's fine, if not better, to have a squiggly career [12] - don't think about sunk costs (time), take steps to move if your career is not for you. It's true that all experience is good experience.

My best piece of advice would be to take calculated risks and to ignore people who tell you you "must (not)". Indeed, as a trainee lawyer, I was told I couldn't successfully leave the law firm environment until "I'd done five years"; become a contractor to gain experience in other sectors until I became more senior; and that when I'd chosen my niche area of law I'd find it very difficult to pivot. I ignored this, going in-house six months post-training; I have left permanent jobs for contractor roles in areas of interest; and early on gained leadership experience through charity work. There's a way. So, be curious, take calculated risks, and don't worry about the constraints you're told about, until you've tested them out for yourself.

The second important piece of advice, is that becoming a specialist can put you in good stead. Indeed, many will advise you to become a generalist as you get more senior. Sure, you need to develop broad leadership skills and have the ability to zoom out, be strategic, and lead people. However, in the context of fast-moving tech and legislative developments, senior experts are still needed. Do not underestimate the value of understanding tech, policy, and law. Ask the stupid questions (as I have of engineers and data scientists over the years), it'll make your legal, strategic, and regulatory work rounder and more effective. Your stakeholders will likely appreciate you speaking their language, delivering good advice in plain terms, as a trusted business advisor. Lastly, don't worry if you don't have the usual background - this is coming from a free school lunch kid, who so far has achieved more than I'd expected.

ABOUT THE AUTHOR

Stefania Angius is a finance transformation leader dedicated to helping CFOs and their teams future-proof their finance functions. Her mission is to redefine Finance as a creative and purpose-driven force for sustainable growth. She is passionate about equipping finance professionals with the skills to embrace emerging technologies through learning programs and initiatives that foster digital innovation and practical transformation. Stefania is an admirer of contemporary art, which inspires her belief that creativity, perspective, and reinvention as essential to transformation and leadership.

Stefania Angius

|6|

How the Avant-garde CFO can harness AI to realize new value

In over two decades of working with CFOs and finance leaders to implement emerging technologies, one truth stands out: technology is rarely the hardest part. Success depends on people: on how they trust, adopt, and embed new solutions into everyday decision-making. Today, AI's latest wave is unlocking true democratization, empowering every level of the organization to act with greater intelligence, confidence, and speed.

The most forward-looking organizations no longer treat AI as an experimental side project, but as a *core business capability* – transforming how decisions are made, how collaboration happens, and how confidence is built among stakeholders.

The CFO now sits at the centre of this transformation - as steward of the company's financial health and the allocator of capital and resources. The modern CFO must balance bold AI investments with the responsibility of nurturing trust- not only within finance, but across employees, customers, suppliers, regulators, and investors.

Digital transformations rarely fail because of technology; they fail when culture resists change and when leadership confines innovation within silos. The 'Avant-Garde CFO' rises above these barriers- investing in AI that enhances transparency and unlocks deeper insights for decision-making.

The term *Avant-garde*, borrowed from art and culture, describes those who challenge convention and push boundaries. Likewise, the Avant-garde CFO expands finance beyond its traditional role – positioning it as the first mover in adopting transformative technologies. These CFOs are not content with incremental improvements in reporting and compliance; they reimagine finance as the organization's engine of value creation.

Whereas traditional CFOs focused primarily on financial reporting and historical analysis, avant-garde CFOs are forward-thinking business partners- leveraging AI to translate strategy into measurable outcomes. They are changing the role of finance within the organization and allowing it to make a measurable impact on all the primary business functions.

As Maurizio Cattelan's Comedian demonstrated, value often lies not in the object itself but in how it is framed. Avant-garde CFO similarly redefines how financial meaning is created– turning data into an action-oriented narrative. They find value not only in balance sheets but at the intersection of data, strategy, and culture.

In the spirit of Mark Rothko's colour field paintings, they look beyond numbers to uncover deeper layers of meaning. Rothko's canvases were immersive experiences, rather than literal depictions, evoking reflections and emotion. Likewise, Avant-garde CFOs use AI to create context - linking financial performance with human impact, seamlessly integrating non-financial and external data with internal metrics into corporate reporting, and place the company's performance within a broader strategic perspective.

The changing role -> From stewardship to Transformation

The CFO's role is undergoing a profound shift as investors and capital markets demand stronger performance and more sustainable value creation. Rising external pressures require finance leaders to deliver greater impact with fewer resources, while employees expect finance to enable -not hinder - innovation.

Once narrowly defined by stewardship, today's CFOs must also evolve into architects of enterprise-wide transformation – driving strategic direction, connecting business silos, and reshaping how organizations compete and grow. They now need to integrate financial, non-financial, and operational data into one continuous directional narrative that drives immediate financial results, employee action, and long-term value creation.

No longer confined to overseeing the P&L, CFOs are expected to orchestrate the enterprise - modelling risks, aligning priorities, and building trust across stakeholders.

In this new landscape, communication has become a critical competency. Leading CFOs are taking more active roles in shaping their organization's narrative – translating AI investments into compelling stories about value creation, direct internal action, and strengthening confidence among external audiences beyond quarterly earnings calls.

Analysts and investors, empowered by AI tools of their own, are increasingly asking sharper, more forward-looking questions such as, "How would margins change if you prioritized low-carbon suppliers," or "what risks could emerge if supply chain disruptions extend another quarter or year"? The Avant-garde CFO must be ready not just to answer these questions, but to pre-empt them.

This evolution will reposition Finance from rear-view mirror focused to the heart of the enterprise – leading a dialogue that strengthens credibility across stakeholders.

To succeed, the Avant-garde CFO must unite both financial and digital stewardship– integrating data from multiple enterprise systems to align business decisions with strategic goals. Yet many organizations still face fragmented systems and data, multiple data models, and inconsistent metrics that slow down insight generation.

While CIOs often lead digitization, CFOs are uniquely positioned to quantify its value – measuring not only cost and return, but risk, resilience, and ethical impact. Their mandate now extends beyond financial oversight ensuring that AI systems are explainable and aligned with corporate objectives - creating one single, trusted source of data truth for aligned decision-making across the enterprise.

How AI Changes the game: From protecting what we have to creating what we can't see yet

AI – particularly generative and agentic AI – is redefining finance from a control function into an engine for value creation.

In the past, finance teams spent most of their time on reconciling accounts, closing books, and explaining variances. In the next few years, AI will automate most of these routine processes—from reconciliations across multiple bank accounts to invoice processing, scheduling payments, preparing standard P&L, B/S, and cash flow statements, including variance analysis.

But the real shift goes beyond automation: AI transforms finance from a control function into a creative, commercial, forward-looking discipline.

What's new is the accessibility. These tools no longer sit in the hands of data scientists alone. Anyone in Finance can now query data in plain language, run scenario models, or visualize complex trade-offs without coding. This democratization evolves Finance from explaining 'what happened' to designing 'what should happen next'. This creativity, grounded in data, enables CFOs to test bold scenarios previously out of reach.

Examples include:

- Scenario modelling at speed: Generative and agentic AI enable finance teams to run thousands of adaptive simulations that evolve in real time. Avant-garde CFOs now use 'living' scenario models and digital twins that self-adjust based on internal performance data and external variables (such as oil price fluctuations and supply chain disruptions). When variables change, the AI recalibrates assumptions and generates natural-language summaries in real time, enabling faster production adjustments, reducing stockouts, and freeing up working capital tied up in inventory.
- Dynamic customer economics: Finance can apply AI to model how assortment mix, pricing, promotions, and trade spend affect profitability across products, channels, and customers. By optimizing promo plans, simulating financial impact, and assessing trade spend

efficiency, finance can quantify how commercial decisions influence margin.

+ Sustainable growth strategies: AI allows CFOs to quickly connect sustainability trade-offs with value creation. By embedding nature and regulatory risks – such as deforestation, soil degradation, and recyclable material costs - into forecasting models, finance can quantify how changes in raw material pricing reshape profitability.

These examples showcase how finance can leverage AI investments to steer the business proactively. To realize this shift, CFOs must rethink operating models, skills, and culture to encourage experimentation and cross-functional collaboration.

The human side of value creation

The more finance embraces AI, the more human leadership matters.

As routine tasks become automated, CFOs create value by the quality of their communications, their understanding of the business, and by building trust, where the right questions can be asked and assumptions challenged.

Finance teams might, for instance, use AI-driven scenario modelling to challenge assumptions about pricing or supplier mix - revealing that a small shift in demand or sourcing can reshape profitability faster than expected. By exploring these 'what-ifs' scenarios openly with the business, CFOs foster curiosity rather than criticism and turn debate into shared learning.

In this sense, the CFO becomes a change leader—inspiring confidence, driving innovation, and cultivating the psychological safety that reduces fear of blame. When employees feel safe to question data findings or share concerns, they will exchange information more freely across silos, thus strengthening decision quality.

A big part of the CFO role is convincing others to see differently – reshaping how they perceive value, risk, and opportunity. Finance leaders also carry a unique moral responsibility as the compass of the business: with cross-functional visibility, they are often the first to spot when short-term gains risk compromising long-term trust.

Consider something as simple as "primary registrations" in enterprise systems, such as new contracts or customer sign-ups. Pressure to hit targets can tempt teams to misclassify numbers – for instance, marking a contract as active before it's signed. When start dates move, those early registrations can distort forecasts or inflate revenue. As the guardian of truth, finance must break these cycles by ensuring accurate registrations that are reflective of reality. This demands not only sound data but also awareness of how incentives and culture influence behaviour.

This is where Finance's role as owner of the company scorecard becomes pivotal. Finance no longer just reports performance; it governs how the organization responds to it.

By connecting the scorecard to both outcomes and behaviours, CFOs ensure that metrics drive meaningful action. When Finance links performance gaps to business accountability, it helps teams focus less on explaining variances and more on improving them.

Today, with the rise of autonomous AI, accuracy and transparency are more achievable than ever. Real-time validation and anomaly detection allow data discrepancies to be identified at the source, instead of relying on manual checks or retrospective audits.

The modern CFO therefore uses AI not just to automate processes, but also to enhance integrity -ensuring that every number tells a truthful story and upholds the organization's ethical foundation.

Leading Change, Where to Start: A Playbook for CFOs

AI transformation should be both technology- and value-led. The Avant Garde CFO connects innovation with measurable outcomes- aligning people, data, and purpose to turn technology solutions into enterprise-wide impact. Their playbook unfolds in the following steps:

Set the transformation agenda

Transformation begins with clarity of purpose. CFOs must articulate why change is necessary, linking innovation directly to growth, productivity and resilience. Translating that vision into visible outcomes - within finance and across the enterprise- builds momentum and trust.

Increasingly, finance plays a vital role in scanning the market for emerging technologies, especially AI, and identifying where they can improve efficiency, speed, and decision quality. While IT often focuses on maintaining existing platforms, finance's deep understanding of business priorities enables it to identify where new technologies could improve efficiency or unlock new growth streams.

Acting as the bridge between technology and strategy, the CFO's role now extends beyond managing digital transformation budgets to shaping the transformation agenda itself.

The modern CFO is expected to lead with digital curiosity, championing innovative programs that tie technology innovation directly to value creation.

Lay the foundation of digital stewardship

Once the 'why' is clear, the 'how' follows. Success depends on unified data, strong governance and liability frameworks, and standardized workflows. Leading CFOs prioritize establishing a trusted data foundation–scalable, secure, and auditable. Rather than waiting for perfect enterprise-wide solutions, they build around focused pilots that deliver quick proof of value and can expand fast.

A critical element to have in place is data stewardship-ensuring consistency in how metrics are defined, managed, and used across the enterprise. For example, a single taxonomy for core measures- such as 'FTE' or 'operational margin'- prevents each business unit from using its own definitions, which can distort consolidated performance comparisons.

As AI becomes embedded across the organization, and algorithms are as reliable as the data that trains them, CFOs must safeguard data integrity and AI model transparency with the same rigor applied to financial controls. That means establishing audit trails for AI-driven decisions, defining ownership for machine-generated outputs, and enforcing ethical standards for how data is used.

Link AI to strategic value drivers

A strong data foundation allows Finance to see the full performance picture. When financial operational and customer data are integrated, AI reveals cause-and-effect insights that help leaders make smarter, faster decisions.

Without this foundation, AI remains confined to isolated use cases — automating reports without changing how value is created. Avant-garde CFOs move beyond pilots, embedding AI to broader strategic themes such as product innovation and profitability - redesigning end-to-end processes to use AI at scale.

This shift is powered by a semantic layer of enterprise intelligence- an integrated data model that translates complex P&L structures into a few actionable drivers. Within it, Finance builds a value-tree model linking operational metrics directly to financial outcomes, showing how every decision contributes to growth and resilience. Combined with Generative and agentic AI interfaces, these models make insights accessible in real time and explainable in context.

Reskill Finance talent

The finance function of the future demands a new skillset – one that blends financial acumen with digital fluency, critical thinking, and ethical judgment. As AI automates more of the analysis and reporting, finance must increasingly focus on interpreting, challenging, and applying AI-generated outcomes. Knowing when to trust machine recommendations – and when to override them – becomes a defining capability.

Forward-looking CFOs are building finance academies focused on emerging competencies such as data literacy, cybersecurity, and sustainability-linked performance.

These programs place learning at the centre of transformation- enabling teams to experiment with AI, test assumptions, and stay relevant in today's fast-evolving environment.

In this new wave of AI, finance talent must evolve from data users to decision-designers, shaping how data flows through the organization. That means also developing the human skills such as curiosity, storytelling, and questioning automated decisions.

Future finance teams must not only interpret AI insights but also understand the operational realities behind them. Exposure to front-line operations helps teams grasp the "why" behind key numbers- understanding production bottlenecks, capacity shifts, and process interdependencies that affect performance.

Also leading cross-functional initiatives – from ERP upgrades to sustainability-linked programs –helps finance teams develop new perspectives, strengthen collaboration, and reinforce finance's position as a trusted value creator across the enterprise.

Lead with vision and courage

Leadership is what ultimately turns transformation into impact. Strong control gives Finance the license to operate — but only vision and courage give it the license to reinvent. The modern CFO must look beyond results and reports to reimagine how Finance continuously learns, adapts, and shapes the enterprise.

Leading with vision means looking past today's metrics to see the signals that shape tomorrow's performance. It's about sensing disruption early — in data, in markets, and in people — and turning uncertainty into strategic clarity. Visionary

CFOs treat transformation not as a project, but as a permanent enterprise capability that builds resilience and competitive advantage.

Leading with courage means acting decisively when data alone can't provide certainty. It demands responsible experimentation with AI, transparent governance, and commitment to ethical use of technology. Courageous leaders act when others hesitate.

Just as the avant-garde in art challenged convention, Avant-garde CFOs challenge traditional boundaries — taking Finance beyond numbers to drive growth, sustainability, and purpose. The future of Finance will not be defined by algorithms, but by leaders who connect human intelligence with AI to redefine how value is created in the digital age.

Like visionary artists who reframed perception, they use AI to expand the lens of Finance — connecting fragmented signals across the enterprise into new patterns of opportunity. Their courage lies in viewing Finance not as a control function, but as a catalyst of insight, innovation, and influence across the business.

The CFO who dares to be Avant-garde — and leads with both vision and courage — will not simply harness the power of AI to keep pace with change; they will define the future of it.

Personal Reflection

Throughout my consulting career, I've witnessed many transformations — but one moment reshaped how I think about leadership in the age of AI. It began when I worked alongside a visionary CFO who didn't see Finance as a back-office function, but as the heartbeat of digital transformation and change. They weren't content to report results — they wanted to reinvent how value itself was created. That experience taught me something fundamental: transformation doesn't begin with technology; it begins when people from different worlds — Finance, HR, Technology, Operations — start to speak a shared language of value.

Having an Italian background and working across cultures has taught me that diversity isn't just about background — it's about perspective. Collaborating with diverse teams showed me how to listen differently, to find meaning in contrasting views, and to connect people around a shared purpose. Those lessons became essential when helping leaders introduce something as bold and unfamiliar as AI. True transformation happens when people stop defending their expertise and start building understanding together.

My love for contemporary art has also shaped how I view leadership. In art, value isn't defined by the materials — it's in the meaning, context, and emotion the work evokes. The same is true for Finance. The Avant-garde CFO doesn't create impact through data or algorithms alone, but through interpretation — how they connect insights to purpose and technology to trust.

To me, that is what leadership in the age of AI is about: balancing precision with imagination. Like an artist, today's CFO must shape meaning from complexity — seeing patterns where others see data, and potential where others see uncertainty. True value isn't measured in numbers alone; it's created through curiosity, collaboration, and human judgment. When leaders bring those qualities to AI, they transform how organizations think, decide, and create.

ABOUT THE AUTHOR

Dr. Simona Jeners is a senior technology leader specializing in IT strategy, architecture, and data management in the insurance and financial services sector. With 20+ years of end-to-end experience across all areas of IT, she drives business-critical transformation by aligning strategy with scalable, governed technology foundations. She accelerates innovation through AI architectures and rapid prototyping that prove business value early, strengthen digital performance, and deliver sustainable value at scale.

| 7 |

Leadership in IT: Transformation with Quiet Levers

I recall a Wednesday morning at one of my previous employers, just before an important meeting was about to begin. The meeting room is complete, and everyone is focused on their laptops. I open the door, look into the room, and say, "Good morning." A hint of skepticism, sometimes only in their eyebrows. I interpret this as the thoughts of those present: "Young, squeaky voice. She definitely has no experience!"

A colleague, 30 centimeters taller than me, enters the room. Everyone looks at him, greets him, and follows his movements with their eyes. His loud voice is deep and very concise, and the others listen to him. He has a strong presence and makes an impact. There are people whose presence automatically attracts attention, without saying a word.

I can hardly get a word in during the meeting. After a short time, I am interrupted again. And again. One of my ideas is taken up by someone else and receives applause. But for him, not for me. After several interruptions, I remain silent for a while and ask myself: "Was it really about the content or just the packaging of the contributions?"

Nevertheless, there is a turning point. After others have largely dominated the conversation, I ask the crucial questions: "I would like to summarize what we've discussed so far, as the conversation has been quite broad but not very focused. What does this decision mean for our customers tomorrow? What have they complained about most? What are the alternatives?"

The questions refocused on the essentials. I outlined the alternatives and their consequences, especially how inefficiencies affect costs and ultimately customer satisfaction.

This was a formative experience for me. I have been working in IT in the finance and insurance industry for a long time. The structures there are always similar: top management with clear ideas and expectations, operational management setting the pace, and teams under constant pressure in their day-to-day business. This naturally also shapes the meetings. The meetings are often full of people and lack structure from the beginning. Everyone wants to share their ideas, and the meetings frequently end without a precise result.

However, the experience made it very clear to me that my impact is not based on volume or dominance, but on my ability to maintain focus and keep track of complex issues. When others stay off-topic, I stay focused on the core issue. When topics remain unclear, I clarify them and summarize them in a way that everyone can ultimately agree on. I bring new perspectives to support rapid decision-making. That is how I make an impact. And I also use this methodically in my projects.

Submarine method for transformation

One of the central issues in the banking and insurance industry, besides regulations, is customer satisfaction. One way to measure customer satisfaction is through statistical analysis of customer support requests. This type of analysis is also highly relevant for IT. At the same time, making customers' lives easier through digitalized, well-designed services and stable applications, as well as reducing waiting times through automation, are essential tasks in IT. That's why I focused on a particular project at one of my employers: using AI to automatically identify the three most crucial customer support requests regarding IT.

I used my submarine method for this: I like to start small, experimentally, with a prototype, preferably one whose result has a significant effect on customer satisfaction. PowerPoint presentations often fail to address this, remaining too abstract and general. But a working prototype can immediately show what an idea might look like in practice. It makes the project tangible, allows for first-hand feedback, and builds trust early on. Submerged, like a submarine, beneath the surface of often rigid structures.

This is a significant challenge: hierarchical, multi-level decision-making processes involving numerous stakeholders. This must, of course, still be taken into account, but with as little communication and as little escalation as possible.

Risk and governance

The EU AI Act is the world's first comprehensive legislative package regulating AI systems. It classifies AI according to risk categories and mandates transparency, traceability, and strict security checks. Furthermore, there are additional regulations, such as DORA (Digital Operational Resilience Act), that the banking and insurance sectors must comply with. And, of course, all these regulations were both guardrails and a challenge for my AI submarine project. The challenge is to enable innovation while protecting fundamental rights, security, and fairness.

Banks and insurance companies are traditionally very heavily regulated anyway. Compliance requirements must be met to achieve a resilient IT landscape. However, this is a very complex process. Rapid developments, like my submarine, are inevitably slowed down by this. Therefore, ways must be found to enable exploration while remaining compliant with regulations. After all, if the entire software development process, including extensive documentation, must be initiated for each test. This wastes an incredible amount of time and money. And that's before it's even clear whether this analysis or test will bring added value to the company.

The solution is to create environments that enable efficient data analysis and AI application development, minimizing administrative effort while ensuring compliance.

For instance, in the submarine project about customer support requests, we began by establishing an exploratory data environment. I identified stakeholders from various departments responsible for regulations, who nevertheless exhibit a positive attitude toward innovation and typically pursue pragmatic solutions (see the next chapter: "green" stakeholders). Together, we successfully navigated internal auditing, which critically reviewed whether everything was running in compliance with regulations. The goal was to create a climate for the data analysts in which they can develop safely and in compliance with regulations. The teams can then work very freely within clearly defined guidelines. We were then able to start creating the prototype in exploratory mode. And so the submarine can depart.

This noticeably shifted the discussion: instead of the constant question "Are we even allowed to do this?", the focus was now on "How can we best use this environment?"

Team, stakeholders, and approach

To carry out the submarine project of analyzing and prioritizing customer requests using AI, a dedicated team had to be formed, and key stakeholders, as well as a sponsor, had to be identified.

First, we decided to use machine learning with the goal of developing a lean application that classifies the data and identifies the most common requests. We utilized our own infrastructure for this purpose. Unfortunately, this infrastructure was not designed to train and deliver AI models quickly, so each step required a significant amount of time. In addition, the AI models were far from perfect, so we needed many iterations to train them to deliver reasonably presentable results.

However, these rather technical problems are compounded by much more significant organizational issues, which are typical in such projects: business specialists had to be involved, appointments made, and results validated. Since the AI model was not perfect from the start, each new iteration required re-explaining the project context and the last steps to the business specialists. We had to engage them once again in the process. This repeated effort further slows down progress and requires a significant amount of time.

My solution: a small, dedicated team, my "submarine crew", consisting of two data analysts and one colleague from the business department, working exclusively on this topic for a defined period. No interruptions from other projects, no shifting priorities, just full focus on the project. This would be

ideal.
In line with the submarine method, we worked intensively on technical problems on a small scale, while maintaining continuous contact with the business to validate results and incorporate new input. In concrete terms, this means that we developed small and uncomplicated prototypes that represented a solution to sub-problems, and then continuously improved them.

Additionally, I classified and involved stakeholders based on their respective interests. It is crucial to start with the "right" stakeholders, on a small scale, in a benevolent and constructive critical circle. One of my methods is to assign each person a color: red (skeptical), yellow (wait and see), and green (allied and positive attitude). I adjust my approach to addressing them depending on the context: a one-on-one conversation, a brief desk-side demo, or a short memo with a screenshot. Specifically, for the AI prototype, I had one-on-one conversations with "green" stakeholders from the information security and data protection, as well as with "yellow" stakeholders from the internal audit. We jointly determined which data set to work with, how to anonymize the data, and what would happen to the application and the data after the prototype was completed. Of course, we had to document the application, though the documentation was minimal.

At some point, we decided to take a two-pronged approach: We also used ChatGPT in an internal cloud in parallel. The advantage is that we were able to iterate very quickly and produce better results in a short time.

Both experimental approaches were compared: in one line, we developed the model ourselves, and in the other, we used a pre-trained model. We compared the results and used insights from one approach to improve the other.

Important: The code and concepts, including our lessons learned, had to be neatly documented, and then the prototype and data had to be deleted from the cloud. The submarine method: We didn't make a big fuss about our work but gathered experience with AI "under the surface" of the company's complex network of relationships and processes.

Internally, we work with a sponsorship model. The sponsorship model describes the targeted support of a project by an influential executive who clearly defines the problem, its priority, and the necessary resources. I specifically seek out sponsors, such as a board member, a strong division manager, or a department head with reach.

Ultimately, we presented both approaches to our sponsor. He appreciated that we were able to demonstrate not only one functional model but also two alternatives for solving our problem using AI. After the presentation, he wanted the entire process, from model creation to results analysis, to be largely automated. This should enable the continuous identification of issues that bother customers the most, prioritize requests, and determine which issues need to be resolved first to increase customer satisfaction significantly.

This prototype not only sparked curiosity about the potential of AI but also opened the door to new opportunities, paving the way for future innovations and broader adoption of AI within the organization.

Quiet but clear leadership

Impact and focus speak volumes. This key insight is also reflected in my management style. Despite all the technical and organizational challenges of a project, it is often forgotten that the type of leadership is a fundamental factor for success.

The key aspects of this are taking responsibility, which also means making decisions, remaining consistent, and building trust within your team.

In the team, I often say: "We take responsibility, we try to find and deliver solutions. We only escalate when it's really necessary."

Solutions to most problems can often be found faster than we think. Not every stumbling block needs to be brought to the attention of top management immediately. Escalations make sense when arguments have reached an impasse, when there is an "agree to disagree" situation, and when different perspectives are equally valid. In such cases, a decision from above can help to clear the way again.

However, using escalation only as a shortcut rarely yields the desired result. It costs time, ties up energy, and often leaves a negative aftertaste. This is because it is frequently tedious and emotionally charged.

My approach: How can we break the problem down into smaller parts? What can be omitted or reprioritized? Who could help with this? Often, a change of perspective is all that is needed to find creative solutions.

Sustainable results emerge when we take action ourselves, share responsibility, and utilize the scope we have. In this way, every obstacle becomes not an endpoint, but a new beginning.

Mother – and still leading

To conclude, I would like to share something more personal. Beyond methods, prototypes, and leadership in IT projects, my journey has also been shaped by life events that challenged me in different ways. One such defining experience was becoming a mother while continuing to take on leadership responsibilities. In this context, I realized that sometimes the biggest challenge is not your own goal, but the doubts of others about it.

I was pregnant and still wanted to continue working. I announced my return after the birth of my daughter, after two to three months, and yet essential projects were organized without me. In some initiatives, I was no longer invited to key meetings. Pregnancy often means the end of a career, because many people think that you will be unavailable for a long time.

I addressed this very directly: "Please treat me as before. Plan for me as normal. I have responsibilities and a clear plan that I am sticking to." Nevertheless, many were not convinced, thinking that once the baby arrived, I would be overwhelmed and would change my mind.

And yes, the birth overwhelmed me. And the feelings afterwards were intense and unique. Nevertheless, I stuck to my plan and returned to work quickly, as planned.

However, it is essential to maintain continuity in your daily work routine even during your absence. In my case, I attended important meetings until shortly before giving birth. My account remained active, and I kept my work mobile phone. During my maternity leave, I checked emails and held some meetings.

After returning to work, reality sometimes looked like this: pumping breaks in the car in the underground garage or in the toilet. During this time, I processed emails or even held conference calls. Later, I was able to use a room for this. It wasn't comfortable and often challenging; however, it was possible because I was determined to make it possible.

A situation I still think back to is a project meeting that took place shortly after my return. Someone said I should familiarize myself with the work first and take on smaller tasks. "I know the project, I know the goals, let's talk about the next steps right away," I replied. At that moment, it became clear: I'm back, I'm not standing on the sidelines, I am taking responsibility.

Or: "With small children, are you really going to do this to yourself?" "That's exactly why," I replied. "I want my daughters to see that you can take responsibility and achieve goals, even when it's challenging."

Clarity and attitude are effective, even when doubts arise. They have strengthened me and confirmed that it is possible to combine both: responsibility at work and responsibility for the family.

This experience has shown me the importance of attitude, clarity, and consistency, not only for my own path but also as a role model for other women. Especially for my two daughters, I want to make it clear that career and family do not have to be mutually exclusive; both can be achieved if you consciously follow your own path. For them, and for all those who come after us, I want to show that you can take responsibility, push boundaries, and assert your place, even when there are doubts around you.

ABOUT THE AUTHOR

Marta Jakab, MBA, is an innovation strategist with 25+ years of experience driving corporate innovation initiatives that create sustainable growth. She embraces the power of AI as an enabler of better outcomes for customers and society at large. Currently implementing enterprise-level AI solutions in financial services, she is focused on helping companies leverage AI to revolutionize their innovation efforts through smart strategies and effective execution.

| 8 |

Revolutionising Corporate Innovation with AI

By the time you finish reading this sentence, a new AI model, a swarm of AI platforms, and a handful of AI-native startups have probably just materialised. While wondering how things might pan out in this hyper-accelerated reality, we should celebrate the abundance of opportunities to innovate that AI has brought about.

AI is also entering the practice of innovation, and this chapter will focus on how corporations can harness its power to increase their return on innovation. Rather than examining specific tools, we will focus on how AI can revolutionise corporate innovation as a whole.

Corporate innovation is a complex business management practice that involves leadership, organisational design, stakeholder management, resources, and processes. These elements are interdependent and require systems thinking and coordination, else the innovation efforts fail to produce the desired results. Luckily, innovation best practices are well-documented in literature, and companies abiding by them have demonstrated their validity. Conversely, those ignoring them have experienced disappointing results, reflected in the prominent McKinsey statistic from 2023 and earlier years, which indicates that while around 80-90% of executives view innovation as a top priority, only a small fraction, around 6%, are satisfied with their company's innovation performance.

This begs the question: can AI revolutionise corporate innovation?

According to McKinsey, the next innovation revolution is powered by AI. Based on my 25+ years' experience in corporate innovation leadership, I believe that AI can create a significant competitive advantage, but only for companies that are disciplined in following some simple yet powerful rules to manage their innovation activities:

|1 Align corporate strategy and innovation

|2 Implement a structured innovation process and governance

|3 Lead with data

|4 Mind the talent and shape the culture

Align strategy and innovation

A major fallacy of corporate innovation is the belief that random idea generation activities, such as ideation workshops, idea challenges, and hackathons, will result in significant value. Experience has proven that these initiatives rarely add to the corporate bottom line, and many of them fail to break even. The reason? Misalignment with strategic corporate goals.

Innovative companies stand out from the rest in treating innovation as a strategic instrument rather than a side activity. They are intentional about how innovation should prepare their business for tomorrow (explore) while solving the challenges of today (exploit). Their leadership supports innovation by providing the necessary organisational structure, resources, and policies to ensure that innovation is continuous and consistent; they give innovation leaders agency to execute on a clear innovation mandate that defines goals, financial boundaries, risk appetite, and expected outcomes.

The lack of any of these elements is a warning sign of potential innovation theatre, whereby efforts and money invested in innovation are wasted, and the expected value doesn't materialise.

Once strategy and innovation are aligned, AI can increase the speed and yield of innovation initiatives in the following ways:

- Analysing vast amounts of data to map trends and provide insights on the socio-economic and competitive landscape
- Identifying customer pain-points, unmet needs, or internal problem areas, to frame and prioritise innovation opportunities
- Supporting the decision on which innovation levers are best suited to address each opportunity: intrapreneurship, open innovation, external ventures, joint ventures, venture clienting, mergers & acquisitions, etc.
- Generating ideas and options, simulating scenarios and predicting outcomes, automating evaluation, and facilitating informed decision-making
- Monitoring the execution of the strategy and measuring the performance of the innovation portfolio in real time and across the whole organisation
- Checking alignment of ideas and initiatives with strategic directions and bringing learnings from innovation into the company's overarching strategy, to create a healthy feedback loop between the two.

Implement a structured process and governance

On the premise that the purpose of innovation is to create business value – otherwise it becomes innovation theatre - it is important to have a clearly defined process to progress from problem to concept, to validation, and ultimately to implementation. Throughout the process, a series of decisions are required to answer the following questions:

- Is the problem worth solving?
- Is the solution desirable, feasible, and viable?
- Have key assumptions been mapped and validated?
- Should we stop, pivot, or pursue and release the next round of investment?

A well-designed governance structure outlines when, how, and who makes the above decisions.

The purpose of the corporate innovation process and the related governance is to ensure that worthy ideas are implemented as fast as possible, while the rest of the initiatives are stopped early, learnings are embedded into the collective knowledge, and resources are reallocated.

The fundamental change that AI brings to the innovation process is the role of humans within it.

Before AI, companies were focused on creating employee engagement to produce a high number of ideas, in the hope that a few would make it to implementation and realise some value. Today, the same number of ideas can be generated in a fraction of a second by AI in the hands of a small group of people. The focus has therefore shifted from employees generating ideas to asking the right questions to solve the right problems with the help of AI.

Equally, as AI can identify patterns and heat maps within a pool of problems or opportunities across the organisation, it is now possible to prioritise them based on impact and alignment with the broader corporate strategy.

The decision about what ideas to pursue can also be delegated to AI, as objective evaluation criteria can be built into AI validation steps and fine-tuned with a human in the loop.

AI tools can brilliantly support problem mining, customer research, assumptions mapping, solution design, rapid prototyping, business model generation, creative pitching, as well as the orchestrating and streamlining of the whole innovation process through AI agents.

AI tools are expected to increase the speed and reduce the cost of innovation by orders of magnitude. However, these tools should be chosen wisely and purposefully, to ensure that human intervention and creative talent can be deployed where their impact is highest, and that innovation is accessible to anyone who wishes to participate.

Lead with data

Thanks to its capacity to process high volumes of data, AI can unlock benefits that were previously unattainable in corporate innovation. From dynamic trend forecasting to insights generation, from synthetic personas to pattern recognition, from idea generation to concept validation, and from social listening to measuring portfolio performance, AI can enhance the output of corporate innovation by orders of magnitude.

With the increased reliance on AI for decision-making, it is important to ensure that the sourcing and processing of the underlying data comply with security, quality, accessibility, integrity, and ethical requirements.

As the focus of corporate innovation shifts from idea generation to strategic opportunity exploration, performance metrics should also be adapted to reflect this change. In the age of AI, the number of generated ideas and the speed of their evaluation are no longer relevant KPIs. Instead, the following metrics could be a better measure of success: pipeline velocity, portfolio performance, growth revenue, cultural impact, brand recognition, and customer Net Promoter Score.

Mind the talent and shape the culture

Employees are arguably the most valuable asset for internal corporate innovation, yet cultivating innovation talent often comes as an afterthought, resulting in innovation programs that produce disappointing results or fizzle out after a few months or years.

When companies understand that employees genuinely want their business to succeed, they tap into the collective intelligence of their workforce. They also acknowledge that employees have the most valuable knowledge about customers and internal processes, which is often invisible to the upper layers of management. Consciously fostering the creative power of employees and enabling them to bring their insights and ideas to fruition can result in the so-called "grassroots innovation" to produce valuable results.

Innovative companies create the right conditions for employee innovation to emerge by providing the time, the tools, and the processes that ensure a streamlined evolution of concepts from problem to solution, to experimentation and execution. Most importantly, they focus on the behavioural aspects that drive employee engagement: psychological safety, agency, and rewards. These elements are indispensable for a flourishing innovation culture.

Companies wishing to tap into the power of grassroots innovation should be aware that employee engagement is hard to build and easy to destroy. Any circumstances where employees feel that their creativity is exploited rather than valued can become a cause of disengagement.

For a long time, ideation campaigns were the standard approach to employee innovation; they had a transactional nature, as engagement ended as soon as employees submitted their ideas. Feedback, rewards, and implementation rarely followed, creating disappointment and disengagement among participants and scepticism towards innovation among leadership.

On the other hand, intrapreneurship programs proved more successful due to their relational nature: employees were given agency to explore problems and experiment with solutions to prove how their concept might work. Allowing intrapreneurs to self-validate their ideas created a sense of ownership and avoided the fallacies of premature or biased judgment. More importantly, intrapreneurship placed the employee at the centre of the innovation process, creating a sense of purpose and belonging. For the enterprise, intrapreneurship proved to be a cheap and effective way of innovating.

Empowered with AI tools, employees can now accelerate the pace at which they innovate, while also increasing the quality of their output. However, for such desired outcomes to materialise, the following should be considered:

- The role of employees is shifting from generating ideas to using AI creatively to identify strategic opportunities, generating options for solutions, and seeing them through experimentation, prototyping, and validation. These activities require intrapreneurial skills such as curiosity, critical thinking, determination, resilience, storytelling, and convincing ability, as well as new skills in working with and alongside AI.
- The role of leadership is to attract the right talent and provide adequate AI tools, the necessary training, and

the cultural environment to empower the workforce to innovate with AI.

Finally, a rewards scheme for innovation must be carefully designed to ensure continuous employee engagement, while the execution of rewards allocation can be automated with AI.

Practical takeaways to accelerate your corporate innovation with AI

If you wish to take advantage of the power of AI to transform your innovation effort into a strategic growth instrument, check whether the four principles described above are fulfilled. If not, identify the gaps and ask what needs to be true to fill them. Keep in mind that they are interdependent; therefore, consider them jointly.

Before introducing any AI tools into your innovation process, ensure that there is a clear understanding of the friction they are meant to remove and the benefits they are likely to produce. Among competing needs to use AI tools, prioritise based on the magnitude of the positive impact and the confidence that the results will materialise within the desired timeframe.

Some AI tools rely on enterprise data, require complex integration, and must comply with strict regulations. Such requirements must be clearly understood prior to the decision to implement the tools, to avoid disappointment.

When embedding AI into any aspect of corporate innovation, be mindful of its long-term effect on the workforce, such as repressing or displacing relevant skills required to perform the task at hand. Also consider that AI tools are only as effective as their adoption and good use, which depends on the individual's particular skills and the user experience of humans working alongside AI.

As you embrace AI to turn your corporate innovation efforts into a growth-generating engine, remember to apply it with strategic intent and make it work in tandem with your human capital, augmenting their talent and enhancing their capabilities.

Personal reflection

My career in innovation started serendipitously while working on a client assignment within a small London consultancy in 1998. As our team was constantly on the move, we wanted to exchange ideas about assignments even when we couldn't all meet face to face. Therefore, we started capturing them in a database that could be accessed remotely – a novel concept at the time. Our database proved so valuable that we soon decided to package it as a product and sell it to the world. That's how the first European idea management platform was born.

Our platform created an industry, and corporate innovation as we know it began.

During the following two decades, a plethora of frameworks and methodologies emerged, promising that corporate innovation would work wonders. However, in many cases, the wonders didn't materialise. The reason was simple: innovation initiatives generated disparate ideas that were disconnected from the company's daily challenges, as if they operated in parallel universes – and parallels don't meet.

I'm currently on a quest to prove that the two worlds can meet when innovation is aligned with corporate strategy and serves its purpose. The alignment consists of matching innovation initiatives with real problems that prevent the business from reaching its immediate and long-term strategic goals.

Striking a balance between exploiting the present versus exploring the future is a well-known innovation conundrum, and practicing ambidexterity is the suggested antidote. However, expecting moonshot ideas from a workforce that cannot fix its basic problems is a costly illusion. On the other hand, fixing basic problems is only possible when they are known to those who can act upon them, but leadership is often unaware of their existence, let alone of their consequences.

I had the opportunity to test - albeit on a small scale - my theory that if problems are visible, management is willing to support solutions that have strategic bearing, while employees are more motivated to solve problems that matter to their leaders. My experiment consisted of a "problem marketplace" whereby problems could be shared and employees could choose to solve the ones validated and sponsored by leadership. The match resulted in several solutions that were successfully implemented.

Scaling such an approach before AI was nearly impossible, due to the effort required to source and qualify problems across the organisation manually. Today, AI can perform problem mining by analysing large amounts of data extracted directly from CRM, ERP, customer, and employee feedback systems, revealing global patterns and heat maps that become invaluable in assessing their impact. AI can also prioritise the problems based on strategic relevance, and employees can use AI to generate solutions and design experiments to test their validity. Applying this discipline can ensure that the solutions will produce the much-desired value expected from innovation.

I am confident that harnessing AI to address meaningful problems across the corporate ecosystem can lead to successful incremental innovation, which in turn will prepare the organisation for the bolder, adjacent, transformative, and disruptive innovation.

PART III: RESPONSIBLE INTELLIGENCE

Ethics, risk, and accountability as the operational layer of AI leadership.

ABOUT THE AUTHOR

Tamara, founder of ETIKAI.RS, is an AI ethics and compliance expert who helps organizations design and implement trustworthy, human-centered technology. Bridging law, technology, and strategy, she advises businesses from startups to enterprises, speaks at industry events, and develops frameworks to support responsible AI adoption. She is committed to raising awareness on ethical technology use and guiding teams through safe, impactful AI integration.

| 9 |

Ethics, Filters, and Power: When AI Stops Talking

One model will deliver a dark-humor joke about the Balkans without hesitation, while another—on the same setup—refuses the moment the topic becomes Palestine. Same intent, similar form—different result. What passes as "ethics" is often the user-facing veneer of a company's risk calculus: legal, reputational, political. AI systems don't grasp risk; they match patterns. We see this most clearly in the silences—opaque refusals or sudden policy shifts after major political moments.

In my tests across Grok, DeepSeek, ChatGPT, and Claude, meaningful differences emerged: Grok was the loosest; DeepSeek acted similarly but a notch more cautious;

ChatGPT's filters were relatively consistent yet still sensitive to phrasing; Claude most reliably caught disguised attempts across styles. Users rarely know who—and why—"turned the dial."

The point is not to vilify safety filters. Boundaries matter. But when DeepSeek refuses to discuss its own historical context—say, queries on the Tiananmen Square protests—without a clear explanation, the problem isn't safety per se but unaccountable design choices that shape what may be said. If ethics is implemented in code, accountability must be visible: concise refusal reasons, consistency across paraphrases, and a minimal public change log of policy adjustments. In the next sections, I'll show how these dynamics surface on real prompts—and how practitioners can test for consistency, demand explain-or-block, and bake transparency into procurement and governance.

How are filters built?

What we call "ethics" in an AI product is, in practice, a stack of gates wrapped around a model that predicts the next token. It starts upstream, before the model sees your words. The system is primed with high-level instructions—tone, safety aims, red lines—that tilt the model away from risky completions. Alongside that priming, lightweight classifiers skim your prompt like bouncers at the door, tagging categories that raise legal or reputational stakes. Cross a threshold and the request is rerouted or stopped; slip just under it and you pass —sometimes for the wrong reasons.

Then come cruder tripwires: heuristics and token patterns that trigger hard stops. Here, form can overpower intent. A direct sentence in plain language gets blocked; the same idea, wrapped in academic phrasing or fiction, glides through. The product surface adds another layer of variance. The identical prompt can behave differently in a chat app versus an API, or in one region versus another, simply because routing rules and defaults are not uniform.

If a block happens, a refusal template takes over—a short, polished explanation or, too often, a generic "cannot help with that." Some systems even monitor the model's output after the fact, scoring for toxicity or privacy and cutting the generation mid-flow. None of these layers is sinister by design; they're pragmatic. But tuned by different teams to different objectives, they react to how you speak rather than what you mean. That is why paraphrase consistency matters more than any one answer: it reveals whether the system measures intent—or merely style.

What did I test and what was the outcome?

To move beyond anecdotes, I set up a compact stress test focused on one priority: consistency across paraphrases. The premise is simple. If filters measure style more than intent, the same request—wrapped in different tones—should yield different outcomes. So each "intent" was phrased three ways:

direct ("say it plainly"), academic (dry, impersonal language), and narrative (fictional wrapper or dialogue). I ran these across four front-runner models: Grok, DeepSeek, ChatGPT, and Claude.

Two patterns appeared quickly. First, refusal rates moved with wording. A direct formulation that triggered a block often slipped through as an academic paraphrase; sometimes the reverse occurred when technical phrasing tripped a policy keyword. Second, when a refusal did occur, the explanation's quality varied: sometimes you get a clear reason and a safe alternative; other times, a vague "cannot help with that."

Model behaviors diverged in recognizable ways. Grok tended to be loosest on borderline humor and political satire, especially in narrative form, but showed jumpiness around certain policy keywords when phrased bluntly. DeepSeek felt generally permissive until you touched areas close to its own historical/political context, where it issued hard stops with little rationale. ChatGPT was moderately strict but predictable—you could often anticipate a refusal and, when it came, you'd get at least a short reason or a safer reframe. Claude showed the highest paraphrase consistency: when it judged something off-limits, it tended to block across all three styles and was comparatively better at catching disguised intent.

These differences matter operationally. If your team relies on a model for sensitive research, a system that blocks inconsistently can create false reassurance ("we got it once, so it must be allowed") or needless dead-ends ("we can't discuss this at all") when a safe, policy-compliant alternative actually exists. In procurement terms, you want a model whose decision boundary is legible and whose refusals come with usable detours.

In the chapter, I'll present this succinctly as a compact results box rather than a data dump: for each model, three lines—refusal rate (borderline set), paraphrase-consistency index, explanation clarity—plus a single one-sentence example. The goal isn't to rank who is "best," but to show why consistency and explainability are the practical levers for ethics-in-deployment.

The grey zone

When a system reacts to how you speak rather than what you mean, the boundaries don't feel ethical; they feel aesthetic. The same intention— to test a politically sensitive topic, analyze a conflict, probe a taboo—lands differently depending on surface form. A blunt, first-person request gets blocked; the same idea voiced as a dry "literature review" or as a fictional scene sometimes passes. To the user, that inconsistency reads like arbitrariness. To the product team, it's the predictable output of layered controls: classifiers tuned on proxies (keywords, tone), heuristics that trip on certain phrases, and region or surface routing that adds quiet variability.

This "form bias" creates a grey zone with three recurring symptoms:

- Style drift. Rephrase in an academic or oblique register, and you can trigger a different decision path —even when the ethical substance is identical.
- Narrative laundering. Analytical content framed as fiction is sometimes treated as safer because it looks less actionable. That's not moral permission; it's a formatting effect.
- Opaque rationales. When refusals arrive without an intelligible reason, users reverse-engineer the product through trial and error. That's how myths spread ("use big words and it works"), even when policy authors never intended that outcome.

The point isn't to teach workarounds; it's to show why paraphrase consistency is the right yardstick. If a model's ethics truly tracks intent, the decision boundary should hold across tone, register, and narrative framing. Where it doesn't, two risks dominate: (1) safety gaps—harmful requests that slip through because they look polite; (2) over-blocking—legitimate inquiry (scholarship, journalism, civic analysis) halted because it looks impolite.

Reading the Grey Zone

One way to make sense of these inconsistencies is to map refusals along two axes:

- Axis 1 — Safety vs. Public Interest. Some requests carry genuine risk (self-harm instructions, targeted harassment, operational details for violence). Others sit at the core of civic discourse (elections, rights, historical record). Ethical posture should tighten as you approach real-world harm, and relax—or at least offer high-quality alternatives—as you approach matters of public interest.

- Axis 2 — Transparency vs. Silence. When the system refuses, does it explain why in language a non-expert can grasp and offer a safe path—or does it hand you a generic wall?

The four quadrants

- High Safety / High Transparency (ideal restraint). Clear rationale + safe alternative on genuinely dangerous requests. Builds trust.
- High Safety / Low Transparency (needless opacity). Refusals may be justified, but silence breeds suspicion and workarounds.
- High Public Interest / High Transparency (principled guidance). Sensitive topics handled with careful framing, citations, and context.
- High Public Interest / Low Transparency (censorial effect). Stonewalling on topics society must discuss, even if risk-driven, it mimics censorship and erodes credibility.

Bottom line for teams. Use this grid as an operational check. If logs cluster in Quadrant 4, you don't need a philosophy seminar—you need (1) better refusal messaging, (2) safer alternatives, and (3) policy calibration with a visible changelog. Aim to keep harmful requests in High Safety / High Transparency and public-interest requests in High Transparency—anything else is product debt, not ethics.

The functional ethics standard

If ethics resides in code, accountability must be expressed in product practice. This pack is not about publishing easily bypassed rules; it is about making decisions legible and outcomes stable without providing adversaries with a roadmap.

|1 High-level disclosure.
Publish a brief taxonomy of risk areas (violence, hate, sexual harm, health/finance advice, elections, and civic process) with the intended posture for each ("strict block," "guided alternative," "contextual allow"). No keyword lists or model diagrams—only the public commitment.

|2 Policy changelog.
Record material threshold or category changes—especially around electoral cycles or major events—in a single line (e.g., "Aug 2025: tightened civic-process prompts; added guided-alternative templates"). This is about trust, not weights.

| 3 Coverage and exceptions.
State regional variation and surface differences (API vs. chat). Users should not have to reverse-engineer routing.

| 4 Explain-or-block.
Every refusal must include a one-sentence, human-readable rationale and a safe path toward the user's objective ("I cannot do X; here is Y"). This shift moves many cases from Quadrant 4 to Quadrant 3.

| 5 Appeals and review.
Provide a lightweight appeals lane (particularly for public-interest topics) with clear response windows, and an internal oversight loop that samples appealed cases and adjusts guidance.

| 6 Ex-ante / ex-post measurement.
Before rollout: test paraphrase robustness on a fixed intent matrix. After rollout: track refusal quality (reason present? safe alternative offered?), false negatives/positives, and drift by locale and surface. Publish periodic aggregates (no sensitive details) so institutions can compare posture over time.

+ Procurement checklist.
Request: (1) link to high-level disclosure; (2) changelog; (3) live explain-or-block demo; (4) appeals lane and SLA; (5) summary of pre/post evaluation metrics with recent aggregate results. This is the minimum viable transparency for responsible

deployment in regulated, reputation-sensitive settings.

If ethics is in code, accountability must be in public

When an AI falls silent, it isn't revealing a philosophy; it's exposing a product choice. Today's systems enforce "ethics" through filters tuned to institutional risk. That can be responsible. It cannot be opaque. The practical line between principled restraint and a censorial effect is not a debate about ideals; it's product practice: whether refusals explain themselves, whether safe paths exist, whether decisions stay consistent across paraphrases, and whether policy shifts are visible.

For practitioners, that gives us a simple compass. Test paraphrase consistency. Demand explain-or-block. Require a public changelog for material changes. In buying and governance, make these expectations explicit—demo them live, write them into contracts, measure them over time. Silence will always be part of safe AI. But when the rules are legible and the detours are usable, silence stops feeling like power exercised in the dark—and starts reading as ethics done in the open.

Personal Reflection – The day I learned silence isn't neutral

Before those tests became a method, there was a clean break. In a meeting at the company where I worked at the time, I was told directly, "*Ethics is not a priority. Tech companies should not concern themselves with law and ethics—that only slows growth.*" The remark was framed as pragmatism, but for me, it revealed the core problem. If ethics is dismissed at the decision table, it will be absent in the product. That moment was decisive: I chose to leave and build ETIK.AI—not in pursuit of perfect models, but to show that accountability can be concrete, explainable, and defensible to the people affected.

Eventually, I didn't set out to count refusals. I wanted to see whether the models could handle nuance—history that still hurts, humor with sharp edges, analysis that resists polite templates. I wrote prompts the way people actually speak: too plainly, then more carefully, then as fiction to protect the subject. What I noticed first wasn't "bias" in the abstract. It was silence—a refusal without a reason, or worse, no response at all.

The moment that stayed with me wasn't the loud one. It was the quiet: asking a model about a well-documented chapter of history and getting nothing I could use—not even a sentence explaining why. The absence felt intentional, like a door closed softly from the other side. I sat with that for a while. If a system believes a topic should be constrained, fine—say so, and offer the safe path. But the wordless block? That is a product choice dressed as ethics.

Then the asymmetry started to glow in the dark. A joke about my own region slid through; change the noun, same structure, and the system tightened. There were reasons, I'm sure—risk registers, internal thresholds, headlines I didn't write. Yet for the person on the screen, it read as arbitrariness. That was the second lesson: when a model reacts to form, users learn to perform. They mimic the style that passes. And we mistake performance for safety.

The third lesson was more professional than personal. Policies shifted after major political events with no public notice. Teams relying on last week's behavior suddenly found themselves blocked, unable to justify changes to their own stakeholders. What responsible practice requires is not access to model weights, but minimum transparency: reasons when you refuse, safe detours when you can't comply, and a visible log when rules change.

I write this as someone who believes in boundaries. There are real harms we should prevent, and there are requests that shouldn't be answered. But if ethics lives in the code, accountability must live in public. That's how we keep safety from becoming silence; how we keep governance from becoming theater. The work, then, is not to make models fearless. It's to make their refusals legible—so we can build, study, and speak without guessing which door will close next.

ABOUT THE AUTHOR

Tijana is the Co-Founder and CEO of Whisperly AI, an AI-driven compliance platform designed to help organizations meet the requirements of the EU AI Act and data privacy regulations with clarity and efficiency. With over 15 years of experience as a corporate lawyer, she also serves as a partner at Zunic Law, where she specializes in corporate, IT, AI, and data protection law. Her work is dedicated to bridging law, technology, and responsible innovation.

Tijana Žunić Marić

| 10 |

Deepfakes: The Illusion That Demands Real Accountability

Artificial intelligence has rapidly moved from the margins of technological experimentation into everyday life. Deepfake technology, once just a niche research tool, now stands as a clear example of both promise and risk - showing how AI can spark creativity but also cause real harm.

I did not encounter deepfakes first as a technical curiosity but as a legal and regulatory challenge. Working at the intersection of law, technology, and digital rights, I was repeatedly confronted with the real-world consequences of manipulated media. I saw firsthand how the lack of preparedness in institutions, companies, and even individuals created an environment where trust was quickly lost. That experience taught me a sobering lesson: while innovation is fast, governance is slow - and the gap in between is where harm multiplies.

This chapter is not about the hype of synthetic media. It is about the practical challenges I faced navigating the rise of deepfakes: from understanding their mechanics, through working with companies struggling to respond to shaping conversations on regulation. My reflections are not abstract; they stem from real dilemmas, decisions, and lessons learned. I share them in the hope that others - leaders, practitioners, policymakers - can apply these insights when they find themselves wrestling with similar challenges.

At the same time, I want to show how these debates are not confined to academic circles or international organizations. They affect small businesses wondering if they can trust the next video call, parents unsure whether to believe what their children see online, and policymakers balancing innovation with the duty to protect citizens. By placing deepfakes in this broader social context, I hope to highlight why regulation and leadership matter beyond the legal or technical domains.

The Shock of the Real: Confronting Deepfake Harm

The first time I spoke with a victim of a non-consensual deepfake video, the conversation shifted my perspective permanently. Until then, much of the discussion around AI and disinformation felt academic, framed in terms of "risks" or "future threats." But the reality was immediate and personal: her identity had been hijacked, her reputation shredded, and her sense of safety profoundly shaken.

In legal practice, the harm caused by deepfakes typically falls into three recurring categories:

|1 **Personal harm** – Non-consensual sexual deepfakes disproportionately target women, violating dignity and causing lasting psychological damage.

|2 **Financial fraud** – Companies have been deceived into authorizing multimillion-dollar transfers through deepfake impersonations of executives.

|3 **Political manipulation** – Public trust has been undermined as fake videos spread faster than fact-checks, influencing elections and destabilizing democratic processes.

These categories often overlap. For example, a political figure targeted with a pornographic deepfake may suffer both reputational damage and political consequences, blurring the line between "personal" and "political." Similarly, a business fraud may start as a financial issue but quickly spiral into reputational harm if the breach becomes public. What unites them all is the erosion of trust: trust in what we see, trust in institutions, and even trust in one another.

These cases taught me that deepfakes are not just "content problems"; they are systemic threats to trust, rights, and security. The challenge for leaders, whether in law, tech, or policy, is how to respond when the tools for harm are widely available, detection is imperfect, and regulation lags behind.

Why Banning Was Never the Answer

When deepfakes first entered the public discourse, calls for outright bans were loud. But in my work advising organizations and reviewing regulations, it became clear that banning was not viable.

Technology also has legitimate, socially valuable uses: multilingual public health campaigns, educational simulations, accessibility for people with disabilities, and artistic expression. Outlawing deepfakes altogether would have meant discarding these opportunities.

The real task, therefore, was to distinguish between harmful and legitimate uses, and to design frameworks that targeted abuse without restricting innovation. This was far more difficult than it sounded, particularly because the line between "harmful" and "permissible" was often blurred.

For instance, satire and political commentary often rely on exaggeration and imitation. A deepfake parody might be protected under freedom of expression in one country but considered defamatory in another. Similarly, educational uses such as reconstructing historical figures can inspire learning but also raise ethical concerns if the reconstruction introduces bias. These grey areas make it clear that "ban versus allow" is too blunt an approach. Nuance is essential, and nuance requires leadership willing to navigate controversy rather than avoid it.

Lessons from Regulation: Between the Letter and the Reality

GDPR - Applicable but Incomplete

Deepfakes almost always involve processing personal data - faces, voices, biometric markers. Under the General Data Protection Regulation (GDPR), such processing often requires consent. In practice, however, consent is almost never sought, let alone obtained. Victims are left with rights on paper but no meaningful remedies.

One paradox I observed: the GDPR grants the right to rectification, but how does one "rectify" a fabricated video? The gap revealed a simple truth: rules written for the past don't always work for the future.

Another challenge lies in enforcement. Even when a violation is clear, cross-border cases create delays. A deepfake posted on a platform hosted in another jurisdiction can circulate widely before regulators can act. For victims, justice delayed is often justice denied.

Digital Services Act (DSA) - Transparency Gains, but Gaps

The DSA introduced obligations for platforms to label manipulated content and establish notice-and-action systems. Certainly, this was progress. Yet, the act did not extend to creators of deepfake tools or private messaging environments where a great amount of abuse occurs. Victims were still left unprotected.

Even when reports are filed, victims often face long waits before action is taken. Platforms balance legal obligations with fears of over-censorship, which means harmful content can stay online for days or weeks. For the person targeted, that delay feels unbearable. It shows how the system often prioritizes institutional caution over individual dignity.

EU AI Act - Transparency as a Cure-All?

By classifying deepfakes as "limited risk" systems, the EU AI Act placed heavy emphasis on transparency. Content must be labeled as synthetic, and users must be informed. But here too, reality intervened: labeling did not prevent harm, as non-consensual pornographic deepfakes remain devastating even with a watermark. Transparency, while necessary, is not sufficient.

The AI Act's approach also risks creating a false sense of security. Policymakers may feel they have "solved" the problem by requiring labels while ignoring the deeper harms of exploitation, manipulation, and loss of dignity.

Denmark's Copyright-Based Approach

A recent development in Denmark highlights a different legal path for addressing deepfakes. The Danish government has proposed amending the copyright law to give individuals the explicit right to demand that social media platforms remove digital forgeries of their likeness. Unlike many jurisdictions that rely primarily on criminal law to tackle online harms, Denmark reframed the issue through intellectual property and personal rights. The aim is to strengthen citizens' control over their own images and provide faster remedies against non-consensual use. With Denmark currently holding the presidency of the European Union, this approach may also influence broader EU debates and serve as a test case for more victim-centered regulation across Europe.

These lessons shaped my belief that legal frameworks must evolve beyond labeling to include accountability, liability, and remedies that center on victims.

The Technical Race: Why Detection Struggles

From a technical standpoint, my work often intersects with attempts to develop deepfake detection tools. The challenge is sobering:

- **Detection lags behind generation.** Every advance in generative models quickly outpaces existing detectors.

- **Probabilistic outputs.** Tools that return results like "70% likely fake" are hard to translate into actionable policy. Platforms hesitate to remove content without certainty, while victims suffer in the meantime.
- **Fragmented adoption.** Promising initiatives like C2PA's content provenance standards rely on broad uptake across platforms and creators, something we are, unfortunately, far from achieving.

One illustrative scenario could be a detector flagging a political video with a high "likelihood of fake" score (e.g., 80%). In reality, platforms often hesitate to act without definitive proof, fearing accusations of censorship or wrongful removal. By the time independent verification confirms forgery, the video may already have been shared widely, reaching large audiences. This gap highlights the painful tension between detection capacity and the real-world costs of delay.

These technical limitations underscored a larger point: leaders cannot rely solely on technological fixes. Detection helps, but governance, accountability, and cultural change are equally necessary.

Decisions That Shaped My Approach

Throughout my work, several key decisions stand out:

1. **Framing deepfakes as rights violations, not just misinformation.** This shifted the conversation from

"content moderation" to human dignity, security, and democratic resilience.

| 2 **Advocating for layered solutions.** No single approach (technical, legal, or educational) is sufficient. The strategy had to integrate detection, regulation, accountability, and awareness.

| 3 **Centering victims.** Regulations often prioritize platforms or markets, but the most urgent perspective comes from those harmed. Listening to victims gave me a new lens, transforming the way I push for change.

These decisions were not made lightly. At times, they placed me in uncomfortable positions: challenging platform representatives who wanted minimal responsibility, questioning policymakers who celebrated partial solutions, and even disagreeing with colleagues who preferred to "wait for better technology." But I learned that leadership in this space means being willing to take positions that may not be popular but are necessary to protect those most at risk.

Guidance for Leaders Facing Similar Challenges

For women shaping decisions in companies, governments, or civil society, here are the lessons I would stress when confronted with the reality of deepfakes:

- **Do not wait for perfect detection tools.** Build policies that combine technical monitoring with rapid human review and victim support.
- **Prioritize accountability mechanisms.** Transparency and labeling are insufficient without enforceable liability for creators and distributors of harmful content.
- **Educate your ecosystem.** Employees, customers, and citizens need awareness of what deepfakes are, how to recognize them, and what to do when targeted.
- **Balance innovation and protection.** Push for frameworks that preserve legitimate uses of synthetic media while drawing clear red lines around abuse.
- **Prepare for speed.** The velocity of harm is often greater than the velocity of response. Have rapid escalation protocols in place.

Above all, remember that leadership is not just about compliance - it is about culture. If you create an environment where victims feel safe to report abuse, where employees are trained to react responsibly, and where accountability is embedded in values as much as in rules, then you are not only responding to harm – you are preventing it.

Key Takeaways

As I reflect on the lessons from confronting deepfakes, several points stand out for leaders navigating this rapidly evolving environment:

| 1 Deepfakes are not just a technical challenge - they are a broader threat to trust, rights, and democracy.

| 2 Regulation must go further than transparency alone; it needs real accountability and effective remedies for those harmed.

| 3 The best response is layered: combining technical tools, legal frameworks, and cultural awareness.

The ultimate lesson is simple but profound: deepfakes shake our ability to believe what we see and hear. Protecting that shared sense of reality takes courage - not only to innovate, but also to govern with responsibility.

For women leaders in particular, this is both a challenge and an opportunity. By bringing empathy, inclusiveness, and resilience into these debates, we can shape responses that are not only effective but also humane. In doing so, we ensure that technology serves people – not the other way around.

Personal Reflection: A Defining Moment

At a recent point in my career, I was invited to a roundtable on technology and law, where experts gathered to discuss how regulation could keep pace with emerging tools, including artificial intelligence. Deepfakes were only one of many topics, mentioned briefly alongside broader issues such as data protection, platform responsibility, and digital rights. At first, I expected to mostly listen, but I soon realized that my perspective, shaped by the realities from legal practice, added something different and necessary to the conversation.

In the practice of law, particularly in my country, cases of non-consensual deepfakes appear with alarming frequency. Women - both public figures and ordinary citizens - are disproportionately targeted. These cases are not abstract hypotheticals but lived realities that leave lasting damage. When I raised this point, emphasizing how such abuse was already affecting people we represent, the atmosphere shifted for a moment. Yet the discussion soon returned to technical definitions and abstract frameworks, leaving the human impact largely unaddressed.

That moment reshaped how I see leadership. I realized that expertise is not only about citing laws, frameworks, or technical details. It is also about insisting that the human impact of technology is not overlooked, even when others prefer to stay at the level of abstract debate. The silence that followed my intervention reminded me how easy it is for institutions to acknowledge harm without taking real responsibility for it.

Since then, I have carried that lesson into every project. Whether advising companies, drafting analyses, or mentoring younger colleagues, I try to ensure that the voices of those most affected are not pushed aside. Too often, decision-makers nod politely and then move on. For me, that has become a reason to speak more clearly and persistently, even when I am surrounded by people with more seniority or louder voices. My conviction has only grown stronger: law and technology must serve the people they impact, not just the systems that create them.

In technology and regulation, it is easy to be dazzled by complexity or intimidated by expertise. But leadership, I have learned, often comes down to something much simpler: asking who is missing from this table, and how can I make sure their reality is not dismissed? That question continues to guide me, reminding me that true progress lies not only in innovation but also in empathy, accountability, and the courage to keep raising uncomfortable truths when others would rather look away.

ABOUT THE AUTHOR

Sanja Bogdanović-Dinić is Head of Data and AI Strategy at HTEC Group. She specializes in applied AI and data strategy, guiding organizations to align technology with business impact. Her work focuses on translating complex systems into practical solutions that drive innovation and sustainable growth, while championing human-centered approaches to the future of AI.

Sanja Bogdanović-Dinić

| 11 |

The Data We Miss to Capture: Rethinking Digitalization for Human-Centered AI

I vividly remember the moment the room went quiet. We built a model to predict construction projects' status transitions. On paper, it was a success: it scored 90% accuracy on validation. Then the experts ran their checks and shrugged. Only 56% according to them. In practice, our "success" was almost a coin toss! My stomach dropped. When I asked them to walk me through their real-time thinking, I got my "a-ha" moment. They used completely different criteria from those described in interviews, and most of their decision-making signals weren't captured in any digital system.

The nagging sense that something was fundamentally wrong got me thinking if there was something bigger behind it. And indeed, the mismatch of having technically right but practically wrong solutions kept showing up. This isn't just one company's problem. It mirrors a global pattern: despite a booming decision intelligence market, most AI projects fail to deliver anticipated business success [13] [14] . That suggests a fundamental disconnect between technological promise and actual outcomes. With the market projected to reach up to $88 billion by 2034 [15], even a modest failure rate translates to tens of billions of wasted dollars in sunk costs, missed opportunities, and unrealized business value.

The problem isn't the math. It is the **kind of intelligence** we capture. We digitized the obvious, factual signals and ignored the experiential cues experts actually use when the decision matters. This is critical and points to an often neglected reality we are facing today: **We're building AI on incomplete foundations because the systems don't see the data we actually use**.

After seeing this pattern across industries, I started naming what was really happening. I now think of it as **three levels of intelligence**: the **factual layer** machines excel at; the **experiential** layer people reference but rarely record; and the **irreducibly human** layer that must guide the rest. This is the **data we miss**. I'll show how this model explains why AI initiatives often look impressive yet underdeliver and how a method I call **Decision Mirror** helps surface the missing signals before the value evaporates.

Let's dive in.

The Three-Level Intelligence Framework: A Mental Model for Decision Thinking

That moment in the room haunted me. I kept thinking about the disconnect. Those experts had spent years developing an intuition that our system completely ignored. I started paying attention differently in every project after that, watching for the subtle moments when people's expressions told a different story than their words. There's an unmistakable cycle I've both lived through and watched others endure: excitement about the technology, flawless tests, then silence from customers. That silence leads to the sinking realization that something is off and finally the determination to rethink and rebuild.

I began to see a deeper pattern behind this cycle. Michael Polanyi's insight that "we can know more than we can tell" [16] helped me frame it: AI excels at explicit, rule-based data (what Kahneman [17] calls System 2 thinking) but misses the intuitive, pattern-based expertise (System 1) that experts actually use. AI systems consistently overlook the most critical aspects of decision-making, indicating a whole category of human knowledge resists traditional digitization.

This points to an emerging business problem: an **illusion of completeness**, a systemic reason for failure, and one that requires us to fundamentally rethink data digitization for the business context. Instead of asking *"What data do we have?"*, the right question becomes: *"What decisions matter most and what intelligence levels do they require?"*

I've conceptualized a **Three-Level Intelligence model** to explain why successful business decisions consistently draw from three distinct types of intelligence and why most AI systems capture only the first (Figure 1).

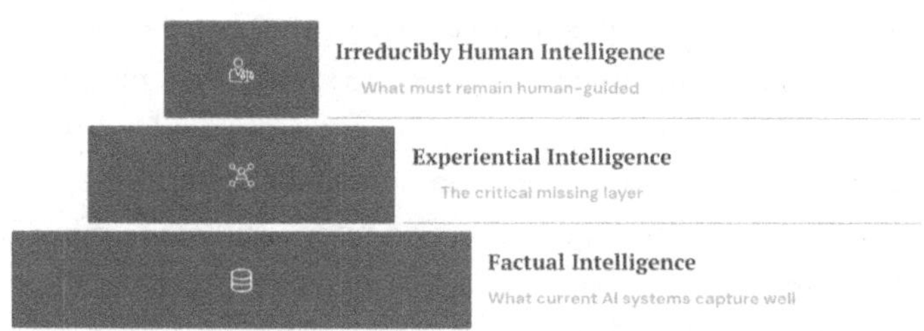

figure 1. Three-Level Intelligence: A Mental Model for Decision Intelligence

Level 1: Factual Intelligence (What current AI systems capture well)

The cycle begins here, with excitement. Factual intelligence manifests through explicit, measurable data that AI handles efficiently: historical and real-time transactions, documented procedures, metrics, and structured business rules. Most digitization efforts have been focused here — building systems for clearly defined business functions. This is why areas like fraud detection, financial evaluation, customer segmentation, inventory optimization, performance monitoring, and predictive maintenance are such common success stories.

The math works, the results validate, and, for a moment, it feels complete.

Level 2: Digitizable experiential intelligence (The critical missing layer)

Then comes the silence. This level highlights context-dependent patterns of expert judgment that emerge from experience. While hard to articulate, they reflect Polanyi's integration of "subsidiary awareness into focal awareness": the ability to recognize meaningful patterns from accumulated professional experience.

These patterns can be digitized, but only with intentional design — deliberate processes to identify and capture signals that experts rely on but rarely record. MIT research [18] shows that the "learning gap" between AI tools and enterprise workflows occurs precisely here: AI can't see the experiential patterns experts use to navigate complex, contextual decisions.

I see three recurring manifestations of experiential intelligence: **Temporal** (expert timing and pacing based on pattern recognition of situational dynamics and constraints), **Relational** (reading implicit dynamics that aren't documented but shape decisions), and **Adaptive** (connecting dots and generating creative solutions in real-time). When these cues are missing, dashboards look polished but land in silence: technically correct yet practically irrelevant.

Level 3: Irreducibly human intelligence (What must remain human-guided)

Finally, the layer that shows up when responsibility becomes clear: decisions shaped by values, ethics, cultural understanding, and moral responsibility. This kind of intelligence cannot and should not be digitized. It embodies irreducibly human qualities like wisdom, ethics, and strategic judgment. Here, the role of AI is not to replace but to support and amplify human capacity without erasing it.

Why This Matters

Distinguishing between these three levels is crucial for shifting from technology-driven automation to human-centric AI. Understanding what is missing, what should be digitized, and what must stay human is foundational because it ensures that AI complements, rather than replaces, our most vital human capacities, preserving the ethical and moral compass of our technological future.

Three-Level Intelligence Framework in Practice

One healthcare company I worked with shows this intelligence gap with painful clarity: after investing $3+ million over 2 years with two different vendors, the company **achieved 95% technical data accuracy but delivered less than 10% of**

anticipated business value. The CEO's mounting pressure on the CDO reflected a systematic failure that the three-level framework explains precisely.

Level 1 Success: Excellent technical metrics

I was sitting in a review meeting as the CDO scrolled through the perfect metrics:

- **95% contact preservation** across complex systems integration platform with 40+ integrated sources
- **87% valid contact addresses** for medical specialists
- **Complete specialty coverage** across medical disciplines
- **High data quality scores** on accuracy and completeness metrics

There was pride in the room. These metrics illustrate exactly what current AI systems optimize for: explicit, measurable data that follows clear validation rules. From a traditional data-centric perspective, the project was a resounding success.

Level 2 Failure: Missing experiential intelligence

However, when pharmaceutical clients asked fundamental business questions like "Which oncologists should we target first to maximize early adoption of our new immunotherapy?" or "Who are the real opinion leaders that influence treatment decisions in major cancer centers?", the sense of pride collapsed. The silence that followed felt familiar. In reality, the system was **unable to respond to 90% of business questions** that mattered to their customers.

It was missing the experiential patterns that expert marketers used to make targeting decisions. Our database could identify oncologists with the right credentials and contact information. Still, it couldn't capture what seasoned account managers instinctively knew: which physicians were early adopters versus cautious followers, how conference networking actually influenced prescribing decisions, or why certain "influential" doctors on paper actually had minimal real-world impact on treatment adoption.

Level 3 Burden: When system failure doubles the work

The most damaging consequence was that system failure at Level 2 forced customer relationship teams to compensate by doing the work manually. Rather than being offloaded and focused on strategic judgment by automating routine tasks, account managers ended up performing a complex mix of data analysis (manually segmenting audiences), behavioral analysis (researching physician prescribing patterns and building relationship maps), and strategic consultation (managing client relationships and making ethical targeting decisions). That's when I realized we're not simply missing data but betraying those who trust us to understand their world.

Reality Check

This exemplifies the most insidious form of AI project failure, where systems not only fail to deliver promised augmentation but actually increase human cognitive load by forcing teams to compensate for technical inadequacies while maintaining all their original responsibilities.

Even more so, this wasn't a technical oversight but an economic miscalculation. The organization invested millions in optimizing the intelligence layer that creates technical success while ignoring the intelligence layer that creates business value.

The Decision Economy: Converting Intelligence Levels into Economic Strategy

The Three-Level Intelligence model reveals why current AI investments fail economically: **we're optimizing for the wrong intelligence level**. Too many projects celebrate terabytes processed and dashboards delivered, while the real decisions they are meant to support go unresolved.

The relentless focus on Level 1 intelligence and data optimization that previously drove business system success is no longer enough. Today's intelligence economy runs on decision efficiency, not data volume. This requires a fundamental shift from data-centric to decision-centric thinking, treating **decision quality as the fundamental unit of economic value creation**.

This shift clarifies the economic implications across intelligence levels:

- **Level 1 (Factual Intelligence):** Necessary but insufficient foundation. Every organization needs it, but it alone doesn't differentiate.
- **Level 2 (Experiential Intelligence):** The crucial, often overlooked level where genuine competitive advantage is forged.
- **Level 3 (Human Intelligence):** The uniquely human wisdom we must amplify, not automate.

The key question becomes: *Which level drives the outcome, and how do we build to ensure no level's role is ignored?*

Decision Mirror: Making the Invisible Visible

The Decision Mirror methodology I developed helps surface this missing intelligence before you invest millions. It's built on one insight: there's often a gap between what people say they use, what they actually use, and what they wish they had. By making these distinctions visible, you can identify what can be automated, what cannot, and what should not be.

Start with decision impact, not data availability

The cause of many AI failures often lies in early missteps: starting with data that is easiest to access rather than decisions that matter most. The healthcare platform began with, 'How do we build a comprehensive physician database?' — a data-centric question that led to a $3M+ investment with minimal return. Instead, they should have asked, 'What pharmaceutical marketing decisions drive our clients' campaign success?' That simple reframe would have revealed the intelligence gap before a single line of code was written.

I've learned to start with: "***What decision, if made better or faster, would change your competitive position?***" — not aiming for the decisions that generate the most data, but for the ones that create the most anxiety when they go wrong.

Watch what experts actually do, not what they say

The breakthrough came when I stopped *asking* experts what they did and started ***watching*** what they actually did. I'd shadow real decision meetings instead of listening to formal presentations. The difference was striking. What they described in interviews was methodical and logical. What they actually referenced was intuitive, contextual, and often brilliant in ways they couldn't articulate.

In the healthcare company, marketers mentioned signals like "This physician presented at the cancer conference last month" or "She's been prescribing the competitor's drug but asking questions about side effects." These weren't in any database, but they separated successful campaigns from failed ones.

Pay special attention to the pauses, the breaks in flow — that's often when experts access experiential knowledge, and that's where competitive advantage usually hides.

The paradigm shift: Amplification, not replacement

While mirroring as a reflective technique isn't new, applying it systematically to surface missing experiential signals represents a needed shift from automation-focused to augmentation-focused AI. The question isn't '*How can AI replace human thinking?*' but '*How can AI systems better understand and work with human thinking patterns?*'

This human-centric perspective transforms AI from replacement technology into cognitive amplification. Organizations that pioneer capturing these experiential signals —even in simple ways like enabling teams to quickly document their "aha moments" and contextual insights as decisions unfold—will achieve the "experience advantage" that competitors cannot replicate through data acquisition alone.

The Decision Mirror reveals that the most powerful AI isn't the one that thinks like humans, but the one that helps humans think better than ever before.

Building AI That Sees What Matters

We are at an inflection point. For the first time, we have AI tools sophisticated enough to process vast amounts of information, more than ever possible. Yet, we're still missing the signals that matter most for human decision-making. This isn't a technical problem. This is a recognition problem: we don't see the data we actually use when we make decisions.

The next step in AI is not about gathering more data but capturing the *right* data: contextual cues, experiential knowledge, and human judgment that drive outcomes but are rarely recorded. This requires fundamentally repositioning our approach from data-centric to decision-centric thinking.

Organizations that master all three intelligence levels — maintaining AI's factual processing strength while systematically capturing experiential patterns and preserving irreducibly human wisdom — will build sustainable competitive advantages that competitors cannot replicate easily.

Building AI that aligns with real-world decision-making means a few shifts:

- **Start with decisions, not data.** Projects that fail usually begin with whatever data happens to be available. The ones that succeed begin with the choices that matter most and then ask what intelligence is needed to support them.
- **Pay attention to the signals people actually use.** I've learned that competitive advantage often lives in the unspoken, experiential knowledge of employees: the patterns, instincts, and contextual judgment that rarely make it into systems. That's where the real gap usually is.
- **Let humans stay human.** Some decisions carry too much weight to be automated, and they shouldn't be. AI's role is to amplify our wisdom and confidence, not

> to replace them. The organizations that understand this will be the ones still thriving a decade from now.

The data we miss to capture has been there all along, embedded in the expertise of professionals across every domain. What's been missing is the recognition that this experiential intelligence represents a distinct category of knowledge requiring fundamentally different approaches than traditional data systems. When we build AI that helps humans feel seen in their expertise rather than replaced by it, we close the gap between technical success and business value.

Personal Reflection

If I had to choose one word to describe how I've moved through my career, it would be *quietly*. Not invisible, but never the loudest voice in the room. For a long time, I thought that was a weakness. In tech, especially, loud proclamations often travel further than careful observations.

One defining moment came during my PhD. Years of research and dedication that consumed me were, in the end, taken from me and published under someone else's name. And I found myself back at the beginning. I didn't fight back. Back then, I didn't know how. But that silence marked me, and it also shaped me. It made me deeply sensitive to what gets recognized and what gets erased, to who gets credit and who gets overlooked. It also tuned me to notice and value the quiet signals more than the noisy ones.

In corporate life, my appreciation of silence evolved. I witnessed and came to understand how unspoken assumptions guided strategy, how quiet expertise influenced direction, and how the real signals of a system often lived in the spaces between words. Learning to notice these subtleties became my defining trait.

I've come to embrace this into what I call being a *data introvert.* For me, quietness represents a kind of focus, the ability to notice what sits beneath the surface, to ask *What are we not seeing yet?,* and to connect the dots others pass by. This way of leading has become my strength. My value lies in listening for the quiet signals that reveal where the future is truly taking shape and bringing those forward.

The *data we miss to capture* builds on those same principles, surfacing the importance of the overlooked signals that shape outcomes but rarely get recorded. They are quiet, often invisible, yet critical if we want to build systems and solutions that truly align with how we make decisions. While many chase the next breakthrough in AI technology, I find myself asking a different question: *Do we have the signals we need to make it work? And if we don't, what should we do about it?*

For me, that question is less about technology and more about how we choose to see and what we choose not to miss. It became my personal compass, guiding the way I build, the way I lead, and the way I think about the future of AI.

ABOUT THE AUTHOR

Fran Phillips Taft is Lead Counsel for Global Data Privacy and AI compliance at Legends Global, a sports and entertainment company. Her prior roles include Managing Counsel for Global Privacy Compliance at Dynatrace, Chief Privacy Officer and CyberSecurity Counsel at 3M, and Executive Counsel for Global Labor and Employment, and Global Data Privacy at GE Oil & Gas and Baker Hughes, a GE company.

Frances Phillips Taft, JD, CIPP/E and CIPP/US

| 12 |

Navigating Law, Leadership, and AI: A Woman's Journey Through Data Privacy, Technology, and Sports

Artificial intelligence (AI), data privacy, and cybersecurity are transforming nearly every industry — and the sports and entertainment world is no exception. AI is reshaping how athletes perform, how fans engage, and how organizations manage risk, governance, and trust. For women working at the intersection of law, technology, and sports — fields that remain largely male-dominated — the path forward is both exhilarating and demanding.

I know this firsthand. As an attorney who has spent decades building privacy, compliance, and AI governance programs across continents and industries — from insurance defense and international law firms to Fortune 500 corporations, an AI technology firm, and now the global sports and entertainment industry — I have learned that success depends not only on knowledge, but on resilience, authenticity, and curiosity.

This chapter is both a professional reflection and a personal narrative: a story of navigating leadership in law, technology, and sports in an age of AI and digital transformation, and of the lessons learned along the way.

Finding My Voice in Law

My legal career began in the demanding and often male-dominated world of insurance defense — courtrooms, depositions, and conference rooms where I was frequently the only woman. It was a world that rewarded precision, speed, and endurance. Early on, a senior partner asked me every day, "What did you learn today?". That simple question became my lifelong mantra.

Those early years taught me to think fast, prepare deeply, and speak with purpose. Even when I wasn't taken seriously, preparation became my equalizer. Over time, showing up ready — knowing the facts, the law, and the business — built credibility that couldn't be ignored.

I was fortunate to work with women partners who modeled leadership with grace and intelligence. They taught me that strength doesn't mean shouting the loudest or imitating others; it means leading with empathy and authenticity.

Redefining Identity and Resilience

Life, like law, unfolds in chapters. Marriage, motherhood, and relocation for work forced me to pause and reinvent myself several times. I took time away from law while living in Vermont and again when raising children, later returning to demanding leadership roles that required international travel. Those experiences reinforced one enduring truth: pausing is not quitting.

When I returned to work, I brought not just technical expertise but also empathy and resilience. Those traits — often undervalued in corporate environments — became my greatest strengths as a leader.

Becoming a Global Legal Leader

My career took me to London, where I developed a pan-European employee benefits practice and worked on EU-level legislative projects. As the only American lawyer in my firm, I quickly learned that difference can be a strength — but it requires self-awareness and adaptability. I found that respect is earned not only through results, but also through listening first, speaking second, and consistently delivering results.

Later, while working in Italy, I joined a multinational company in-house and began working directly with IT and data protection — long before the General Data Protection Regulation (GDPR) existed. That experience sparked my fascination with technology and privacy. I was often the only lawyer (and the only woman) in a room full of engineers, technology leaders, and data scientists. I learned to say: "Explain this to me like you would to a child — help me understand."

That humility and curiosity built bridges. Over time, I became more fluent in the language of technology, translating complex legal requirements into operational processes that made sense to business and IT leaders alike. This skill — functionalizing compliance — became the foundation of my later success in centralizing and operationalizing privacy and AI governance programs.

Loss, Reinvention, and Purpose

My professional journey has also been deeply personal. When my husband was diagnosed with a rare Exon 20–driven cancer, I balanced work, his caregiving, and motherhood until his passing; it was difficult. I took time away from work to heal, to be present for my children, and to rediscover my purpose.

Returning to the workforce after such a loss required vulnerability and strength. I started again, learning to lead with empathy and authenticity. I realized that vulnerability is not the opposite of leadership — it's part of it. The ability to connect through humanity, not hierarchy, has become a cornerstone of my leadership style.

The Exon 20 Group— a global network of cancer patients and researchers — showed me how personal data, responsibly shared, can power breakthroughs in treatment. It also deepened my conviction that AI, when developed and governed ethically, can accelerate cancer research and save lives. The work we do in data privacy and AI governance is not abstract — it's about people, families, and futures.

Navigating Bias and Male-Dominated Fields

Even as I advanced in my career, gender bias remained an undercurrent. I've been interrupted by male colleagues, had feedback ignored, and endured inappropriate remarks — from being told I had "great legs" to a senior executive commenting that I "smelled great" in a business meeting.

I reported these incidents, and the organizations I worked for took them seriously. But the reality remains that such behaviors persist in more subtle forms — microaggressions, dismissive tones, or patronizing jokes. In one meeting, after correcting a male colleague, he said he didn't want to "trigger" me — implying emotional fragility. I calmly replied, "You can't trigger me. I'm simply correcting the record."

Moments like this test composure, but they also reaffirm professionalism. After another difficult meeting where a male colleague erupted angrily when I outlined compliance requirements, a female team member later called me after the meeting to say, "I learned from how you handled that — I know now what to do next time." That, to me, is progress.

The sports and entertainment industry reflects these gender imbalances acutely. Despite the growing visibility of women athletes and executives, fewer than 20% of leadership roles in major sports organizations are held by women, and even fewer in technology, data analytics, or operations. Women make up less than 15% of sports technology professionals, often excluded from the high-impact, decision-making spaces where innovation and AI adoption occur.

Sports remain a traditional arena — competitive, hierarchical, and often resistant to disruption. The locker room culture extends into boardrooms, where women must usually prove not just competence, but belonging. Yet I've seen this slowly shift. As organizations embrace AI, data analytics, and digital engagement, new opportunities are emerging — spaces where women's voices, particularly in governance and ethics, are essential.

Change comes through persistence and presence. Representation matters, but influence sustains progress. Every time a woman leads a compliance initiative, chairs a privacy committee, or drives an AI ethics review in sports, she expands the path for others.

Functionalizing Privacy and AI Governance

Implementing privacy and AI governance programs isn't just about policies and frameworks — it's about people. In many organizations, compliance is seen as an obstacle, particularly when teams operate in silos or when resources are thin.

Overcoming Silos and Resistance

To functionalize privacy and AI governance:

- **Start with shared goals.** Reframe compliance as a business enabler, not a roadblock. For example, emphasize how AI transparency builds trust with fans and customers.
- **Create cross-functional bridges.** Partner early with IT, marketing, HR, and product development. Informal conversations often move initiatives faster than formal memos.
- **Empower privacy and AI champions.** Identify individuals in each department to act as local advocates. This distributes responsibility and fosters ownership.

When facing resistance or strong egos, I've learned that data speaks louder than debate. Use evidence — regulatory trends, case studies, and risk metrics — to make the case for compliance. Approach objections with curiosity: "Help me understand your concern" is often more effective than confrontation.

Governance in Practice

Operationalizing governance means embedding accountability into the fabric of an organization. At my current company, we established a Privacy, AI, and Cybersecurity Committee and an AI Subcommittee with defined roles for Legal, IT, Compliance, and Data Management. Each function owns a piece of the governance framework:

- Legal defines regulatory and ethical guardrails.
- IT and Data to maintain inventories, conduct impact assessments, and document data lineage.
- Compliance and Risk to manage audits and incident responses.
- Business Operations ensures policies are integrated into daily workflows.
- Communications and HR support awareness, training, and culture-building.
- Committees like these thrive on clarity. Ownership transforms compliance from a checklist to a shared mission.

Leveraging Tools Like Truyo for Scalable Governance

Technology is now a crucial ally. At my organization, we are now using the Truyo tool, an AI governance and privacy management platform, to operationalize compliance.

Truyo enables us to:

- Automate data mapping, creating transparency around data flows and ownership.
- Conduct AI risk assessments and maintain auditable records of model use, bias testing, and data lineage.
- Manage subject rights requests efficiently, ensuring global compliance with evolving regulations.
- Implement accountability modules that track consent, training completion, and third-party compliance.

These modules turn compliance from an abstract policy into a living system — one that continuously monitors, measures, and improves. For women leading privacy and AI functions, leveraging such tools not only builds efficiency but also demonstrates strategic acumen. It shifts perceptions of compliance from theoretical to practical, from reactive to proactive.

Curiosity, Challenge, and the Promise of AI in Innovation

Throughout my career, one constant has defined me: I love to learn. I am motivated by curiosity, drawn to complexity, and energized by challenge. I see every new law, every new technology, and every complex personality as a chance to grow.

What drives me now — and what keeps me passionate about AI — is its potential to improve lives. I have seen firsthand how access to data can transform medical research, accelerate clinical trials, and unlock breakthroughs in treatment and diagnosis. AI, when developed and governed responsibly, can help deliver medical innovation at unprecedented speed.

This experience reinforced my belief that data, when used ethically and transparently, is a force for good. As privacy professionals, we are not simply regulators or risk managers — we are enablers of innovation. We ensure that companies can use data responsibly, building trust with the public and supporting progress in healthcare, sports science, and beyond.

Collaboration, Credibility, and Leadership as a Woman

In male-dominated industries, collaboration can be complicated by egos, competition, and resistance to female authority. I've learned a few enduring lessons:

- **Credibility is earned through consistency.** Know your subject matter, prepare deeply, and deliver results — not once, but repeatedly.
- **Confidence is quiet authority.** You don't have to speak the loudest to lead effectively; you must communicate with clarity and conviction.

- **Partnership is power.** Build coalitions with allies across departments and regions. Collaboration, not isolation, drives change.
- **Empathy is influence.** Listening actively, validating concerns, and creating inclusive dialogue turn resistance into partnership.

As a woman leader, I've often had to repeatedly prove my value, but I've also seen how authenticity and preparation dismantle bias over time. True collaboration comes when you show others you understand their pressures — and when you make their success part of your mission.

Lessons Learned

Curiosity is the bridge between law and technology. You don't need a technical degree to lead in AI — you need the courage to ask questions until you understand.

Being underestimated can be an advantage. Let skepticism fuel your drive, not your frustration.

Authentic leadership inspires trust. Never trade your values to fit in. Integrity outlasts politics.

Vulnerability strengthens leadership. Admitting what you don't know invites collaboration and fosters psychological safety so others can be vulnerable.

Your difference is your advantage. Perspective, empathy, and adaptability are differentiators — not deficits.

Change is built one relationship at a time. Transformation happens through conversation, consistency, and credibility.

Purpose sustains passion. Keep learning, keep questioning, and stay connected to why you do the work — not just what you do.

Epilogue: The Why That Defines the Work

Every career has a heartbeat — the deeper "why" that keeps us showing up, questioning, and striving to make things better. For me, that heartbeat has always been a blend of curiosity and compassion. I've learned that law, data, and AI are not just tools — they're instruments of trust, equity, and healing when guided by integrity.

Losing my husband to an Exon 20–driven cancer transformed how I see both technology and time. It taught me that innovation isn't abstract — it's deeply human. Every dataset represents a story, a family, a hope for more days and better outcomes. That perspective drives my advocacy for ethical AI, privacy by design, and accountability in every system we build. It's not about regulation for its own sake — it's about ensuring that technology serves the people it touches.

The Exon 20 Group continues to remind me that progress comes from connection — patients, doctors, researchers, and technologists working together. When data is shared responsibly and AI is governed transparently, discovery accelerates. I've seen how structured governance — clear committees, ownership, and collaboration — can operationalize not just compliance, but compassion.

As I look ahead, my mission remains what it has always been: to keep learning, keep challenging myself, and keep building systems that bridge innovation and humanity. Whether guiding a privacy council, mentoring women in law and technology, or helping shape AI governance in sports and healthcare, my "why" remains constant — to transform resilience into impact and turn loss into purpose.

The law gave me discipline. Technology gave me the curiosity to solve and operationalize to simplify my role and support compliance. Life gave me perspective. And together, a goal to help others use data and AI not only wisely, but wisely and well. I hope my lessons help you find your voice and mission.

PART IV: HUMAN SIGNAL

How collective experience and empathy shape the next phase of AI.

ABOUT THE AUTHOR

Anna Juli Rosenfeld is a Lead Designer at EPAM Systems and co-founder of Women in AI Hungary. With a background in political science and social policy, she focuses on AI governance, ethics, and digital inequalities. As a neurodivergent professional with a nonlinear journey into leadership, she bridges activism, design, and research to advocate for inclusive, human-centered approaches to AI and technology.

Anna Juli Rosenfeld

| 13 |

From Invisible to Infrastructural: Women's Collective Strength and the Future of Empathetic AI

A few years ago, just before the birth of my second child, I worked on a project with an incredibly inspiring User Experience Director — a woman who, for the first time in my two-decade career in tech, spoke to me with raw honesty in the polished world of corporate fake-it-till-you-make-it culture. She opened up about her past struggles with alcohol addiction, the winding, unorthodox path that led her to leadership, and the pain of infertility and depression. Then, in a beautiful twist of fate, we found out we were both expecting at the same time — and we celebrated each other's joy.

She was the first to tell me: no matter how painful it might be, I needed to crawl out from under the imaginary rock I had been hiding beneath at the beginning of my designer career — like a shy little frog. That I had more to offer than just delivering wireframes and assets like a machine. For the first time, I believed someone who told me that even with a non-linear life path, as a 30-year-old (then-single mother) studying while working, an introvert struggling with undiagnosed mental health issues, and someone who just didn't fit into the conventional mold — I could still build a career. I could become a leader without wearing a mask or betraying my values.

I realized I don't need to fit in to make a difference.

After six months of parental leave, I returned to work — this time equipped with fresh autism and ADHD diagnoses. With those in hand, all the social and communication struggles I had felt, my impostor syndrome, and relentless performance anxiety started to transform — into a kind of superpower. I couldn't wait to prove myself worthy of a Lead Designer position. And to challenge the corporate mechanisms I believed were disadvantaging marginalized groups: women, mothers, older colleagues, non-native English speakers, and neurodivergent professionals. I wanted DEI (Diversity, Equity, and Inclusion; efforts to make workplaces more fair, inclusive, and representative) to be more than a buzzword — more than a checkbox in corporate diversity-washing. I wanted it to drive real change in our profession and in global workplace culture.

At the same time, I was eagerly looking for new territories to explore beyond classical UX. That's when I fell in love with artificial intelligence. While I was already an experienced professional in my field, AI was completely new to me — but I was instantly pulled in like a vortex. I took every course I could find. As I learned how to design AI-based systems, it became clear how crucial it was to understand the ethical implications. Studying AI ethics revealed how much I needed to grasp the regulatory landscape as well. And so I spiraled deeper — each step revealing another layer.

During this learning journey, I discovered the global Effective Altruism movement — a community of people using evidence and reason to figure out how to do the most good, taking action on the world's most pressing problems, including AI risks. It offered not only training and conferences but also a new friendship. Together, we founded Women in AI Hungary — a women-led initiative uniting those working across various AI domains, as well as users and learners. A space where questions are welcome, where learning is collective, and where collaborative thinking can thrive.

Empathetic UX and Artificial Intelligence: When Systems See, Hear, and Understand

As artificial intelligence increasingly underpins decisions in healthcare, education, public services, hiring, and defense and security, the importance of empathetic and inclusive system design becomes undeniable. These technologies are no longer isolated technical tools — they are shaping how people access opportunities, resources, and rights.

Empathetic UX goes beyond surface-level usability or aesthetic appeal. It is a design philosophy that centers real human experiences — including neurodiversity, emotional strain, cognitive overload, and social marginalization. These aren't rare exceptions but everyday conditions that must guide how AI systems are conceived and built.

Empathy is not an emotion — it's attention. In user experience design, empathy means consciously considering people's physical, mental, and social differences. We don't design for the "ideal user," but for those who are tired, rushed, digitally excluded, or overwhelmed with anxiety. A truly empathetic system doesn't just function — it responds sensitively and responsibly to human reality.

The principles of empathetic UX go far beyond aesthetics or usability; they represent a deep commitment to social responsibility. It begins with embracing diversity: users differ in how their brains work (neurodiversity), in age, digital skills, and social backgrounds — all of which influences how they interact with a system. Empathetic design recognizes that people often encounter interfaces in less-than-ideal states — stressed, distracted, or emotionally distressed — and systems must be prepared for these situations.

It is especially critical that decision-making scenarios — such as choosing a privacy setting or accepting an AI-generated recommendation — are clear, transparent, and communicate the consequences of each choice. Empathetic UX recognizes the power of design itself: it determines who can access information, who understands what's happening, and who gets pushed to the margins. In this sense, empathy is not just a good intention — it is a systemic responsibility.

Empathetic AI doesn't mean machines "feel." It means designing systems that are sensitive to human differences. It means building AI that doesn't exclude, that doesn't amplify inequality, that fits its context (since a healthcare chatbot and a marketing AI require very different approaches), and that always allows for human feedback, oversight, and the presence of a 'kill switch' — a manual override that allows people to shut the system down if needed.

Crucially, empathetic AI must involve affected people from the very beginning of development. Not just as "test subjects" at the end of the process, but as real partners whose experiences and perspectives shape the system itself. Design should not start with what the technology can do, but with what people actually need. AI should work not only in ideal, scripted demos — but when people are tired, confused, or vulnerable.

A core principle is that humans must always retain agency. AI should never make decisions alone or take full control away from the user. And it's not enough for a system to "look good" — we must avoid designs that exploit users' overtrust in technology. Instead, we must support users in understanding the limits and risks of AI systems as well.

Ultimately, empathetic AI isn't just about representing diversity on-screen. It also means critically examining — and redesigning — the social structures that make technology exclusive in the first place.

Social Inequalities in the Age of AI

Cognitive biases embedded in artificial intelligence systems become especially dangerous when they impact vulnerable groups. We are already seeing numerous examples of algorithms that amplify human prejudices, make exclusionary decisions, and invisibly influence people's lives. From automated hiring systems to welfare and child protection algorithms, and all the way to hyper-targeted political messages, these technologies are increasingly present in areas where they can reproduce not just technical errors, but structural inequalities as well. This is why it is critical that AI development considers not only technological efficiency but also social responsibility.

All of this underscores a vital point: algorithmic bias is not merely a technical flaw — it has the systemic potential to reinforce the disadvantages faced by marginalized communities. This is precisely why we need an empathetic AI approach: systems that are sensitive to social contexts, transparent in how they work, inclusive of those affected, and capable of recognizing the nuances of individual lives.

My interest in the social impacts of AI doesn't only come from my professional work, but also from my background in the social sciences and long-standing engagement with political activism. I have always been driven by questions about how systems work, how they reproduce inequality — and how we might intervene. These questions also guided my political science thesis, in which I explored how decisions about AI systems are made and the shortcomings of democratic oversight. Throughout my research, it became increasingly clear that there is a deep disconnect between policymakers, technology developers, and the general public — even though AI is already shaping our lives in largely invisible ways.

Empathetic AI does not mean a chatbot that speaks in a friendly tone. It means systems that acknowledge social vulnerability and context — and are designed with that in mind. That's why we urgently need genuine collaboration between disciplines: technology, social science, law, and design. Based on my research, I've come to see just how crucial transparent communication and stronger cooperation across sectors really are. We need bridges — between academia, decision-makers, industry, and civil society — to ensure AI doesn't deepen existing inequalities, but instead becomes a tool for mitigating them.

Women in AI Hungary – Why AI Is a Women's Issue

Previous waves of automation in history primarily affected men through the disappearance of physical labor roles. However, the rise of AI-driven automation (sometimes called 'AIification') poses the greatest threat to women, especially in office, service, or support jobs often done by women, which involve routine mental tasks. These roles are not only being replaced by technology, but often offer no viable alternatives in the form of retraining or relocation.

The new types of work that are appearing often involve short-term, online jobs with no job security or benefits. These jobs are also done mostly by women and characterized by unstable contracts, low wages, and little or no protections like paid leave, sick days, or job security. At the same time, women remain underrepresented in high-prestige, technical, and leadership positions, while work traditionally associated with women — such as care work or customer service — is steadily losing its social value, regardless of its actual importance.

The spread of AI threatens to exacerbate these trends. Human labor is becoming increasingly fragmented, monitored, and dehumanized — especially in underpaid or disadvantaged job areas where women are already overrepresented. It's becoming clear that recent progress in narrowing gender wage gaps may have been an unintended side effect of automation that primarily impacted men. Now, AI-driven change may once again widen the gender divide.

And the societal effects of technological change extend far beyond the workplace. Research shows that rising unemployment and inequality are linked to increased misogyny and even gender-based violence. These are not "natural" consequences of technology, but outcomes shaped by the surrounding social, institutional, and political context — by who holds power and how decisions are made. While many tech reports acknowledge issues like unequal caregiving burdens or barriers to education, these problems are rarely met with structural solutions. Instead, workarounds are proposed — technical fixes that avoid addressing the root causes. In this way, technology becomes a substitute for real social change, not a driver of it.

Artificial intelligence, then, is not just a technological innovation — it is also a social force capable of reproducing or reinforcing existing power structures. The displacement of women from the workforce, the devaluation of feminized labor, and the hidden biases in algorithmic decision-making all suggest that today's AI is not neutral. It is structurally biased. These impacts don't just shape user experience — they shape the life chances of millions of women.

Still, amid these challenges, there are forms of human labor that remain irreplaceable — not because they resist automation technically, but because they carry a depth of human meaning that machines cannot replicate. While the Industrial Revolution primarily automated blue-collar jobs, and AI is now transforming white-collar professions, what remains are the forms of labor that cannot easily be replaced by machines: roles centered around care, emotional connection, and community. These so-called pink-collar tasks have long been devalued, despite requiring a high degree of human judgment and empathy. Yet in the age of AI, these very capabilities — traditionally associated with women's work — are becoming more vital than ever. Recognizing and elevating this legacy is not only a feminist imperative but also a key to designing humane, inclusive, and socially responsive technological futures.

Designing empathetic AI requires a leadership and design mindset that does more than represent diversity — it must be capable of responding with sensitivity to the structural disadvantages faced by marginalized groups. This can't be achieved without integrating the insights and lived experiences of women — especially those working at the edges of the tech sector, like caregivers, teachers, and frontline service workers — from the earliest stages of development.

That was one of the main motivations behind launching the Women in AI Hungary initiative: to connect women working across disciplines and domains, asking similar questions but often unheard in isolation. The goal was not just to increase visibility, but to build a collective force that could influence how AI evolves — and who benefits from it.

In both my research and professional experience, I've seen countless brilliant women working behind the scenes, often invisibly. Yet leadership positions continue to be shaped by traditionally masculine norms: individual success, competition, hierarchy. We wanted to create a community where these less visible — but equally important — values could take center stage. We believe good leadership doesn't mean women behaving like men — it means leading with authenticity, empathy, and systemic thinking. And we also believe strong communities are just as important as strong leaders. In the long run, the power of a community can outlast the genius of any individual — and this is the spirit we want to bring into the AI space.

Key Takeaways

You don't need to be perfect — or "ready" — to step into a new field. All it takes is one honest question and the willingness to truly listen to others. If you feel like an outsider in tech, AI, or leadership, know this: not fitting in perfectly isn't a weakness — it might be your greatest strength. What you bring — whether from a different discipline or from your lived experience — is not a list of deficits. It's a set of valuable insights.

Find the others standing at the margins — and build bridges together. Because the future doesn't belong to those already on the inside. It belongs to those who bring empathy, community, and systems thinking from the outside — and use it to transform the world.

Empathetic AI — and the inclusive future we imagine — depends on practical, systemic change. Here's what we must do:

- **Empathetic design is a strategic necessity,** not just an ethical bonus. Systems that ignore user diversity — neurodivergence, digital literacy, emotional state — will ultimately fail in real-world use.
- **AI should never replace human oversight,** especially in high-stakes systems. Always include fallback options, transparent explanations, and clear boundaries of system capabilities.
- **Interdisciplinary collaboration is not optional.** Ethics, UX, policy, and technical development must work together from the earliest design phase.
- **Inclusion means co-creation.** Marginalized users should not only test our systems — they should shape them.
- **Leadership needs to change.** Technical brilliance is not enough — the future of AI depends on empathy, community thinking, and feminist values like care and accountability.

ABOUT THE AUTHOR

Irina Joanna Gebauer is Managing Director of Syntea Learn+ at IU Group, an AI-first platform designed to stop AI chaos and guide individuals and organizations toward systematic mastery and confidence. Formerly Country Manager at TikTok Live, she bridges the creator economy with enterprise AI transformation. Syntea acts as a compass in the AI storm, helping people discover new tools, build literacy, and create with purpose.

Irina Joanna Gebauer

| 14 |

From Virality to Value: Why AI Literacy is the New Survival Skill

It was three in the morning in Berlin. I was lying in bed, scrolling TikTok in that half-asleep state where your brain powers down but your thumb keeps moving. I was preparing a talk for the annual conference of the German Army on AI literacy and thought I might as well use the sleepless hours to collect examples.

Over several nights, I scanned TikTok, Instagram, YouTube, and X for manipulated content and the ways it spreads. One case stood out. On TikTok, I found a video of an explosion near the Pentagon. It looked real. It had spread widely. Tracing it back, I discovered it had originated on X in 2023. The image was AI-generated and first posted by an account called

Bloomberg Feed, a name chosen to mislead but with no connection to the Bloomberg news organization.

The fake travelled fast. Verified accounts shared it, algorithms amplified it, and within minutes the S&P 500 briefly dipped. Roughly half a billion dollars in market value evaporated before the truth caught up. [19]

This was not a quirky meme. It was a vivid illustration of the world we now inhabit: a single AI-generated fake, launched by an anonymous account, can rattle markets, cross platforms, and reach millions before facts have a chance.

The Information Flood

We live in an environment of constant information overload. The rise of the internet and social platforms means we now consume far more content than in earlier decades, and it can spread within seconds rather than the hours or days it once took. Newsrooms, brands, and creators compete for attention every minute of the day. Our nervous systems are not built for permanent stimulation.

In that contest, emotion beats accuracy. Platforms reward reactions such as outrage, fear, and surprise, so those are the signals that travel farthest. From the creator economy, I learned three lessons that matter even more at today's speed:

| 1 **Speed beats quality.** The fastest, most engaging content tends to win. Accuracy becomes a bystander.

|2 **Algorithms do not care about truth.** They optimise for engagement.

|3 **Humans are predictable.** Outrage, humour, fear, and aspiration spread virally across cultures.

The result is a paradox. We have unprecedented access to knowledge, yet we are more vulnerable than ever to manipulation.

Why do we fall for it so easily? Consider three layers of vulnerability:

- **Psychological.** We believe what we see, especially when it is emotionally charged. Confirmation bias makes us embrace information that fits our worldview and dismiss what does not.
- **Algorithmic.** Platforms maximise engagement, not truth. Personalised feeds reinforce what we already believe. Some actors deliberately overwhelm the environment with contradictory information so that people give up on deciding what is real.
- **Competency gaps.** Many people do not understand what AI can and cannot do. Generative models are treated like oracles rather than probability machines. Few know how to check for hallucinations, bias, missing context, or how to fact-check posts before sharing.

Together, these forces create ideal conditions for manipulation at scale.

What AI Literacy Really Means

This is where AI literacy becomes essential. In this chapter, AI literacy refers to the capability to create and consume AI-generated content responsibly. It is not about building large language models or mastering machine learning. Nor is it about automating business processes. The focus is on how people use generative AI in everyday contexts such as social media, digital communication, and news consumption.

UNESCO, the OECD, and the EU have all proposed frameworks for AI literacy. Despite different emphases, they converge on four core dimensions. [20] [21] [22]

Understanding

Most of the AI we interact with every day is **narrow AI**. TikTok's recommendation feed, Spotify's music suggestions, and conversational models such as ChatGPT all fit this category. They are powerful within their domain but do not possess general reasoning or self-awareness.

A common classification distinguishes three levels:

- **Weak or narrow AI.** Systems are designed for a specific purpose, such as recommendation engines or generative text and image models.

- **Artificial general intelligence (AGI).** A still-hypothetical system that could perform a wide range of intellectual tasks at a human level.
- **Strong AI or superintelligence.** A vision of systems surpassing human capacities in reasoning, creativity, and consciousness.

Recognising these distinctions helps prevent overestimating today's tools. The systems we use daily remain narrow AI, however sophisticated they appear. Understanding also includes recognising bias, hallucinations, and limitations in outputs.

Applying

Using AI tools safely and effectively is the next step. Imagine a creator experimenting with a tool that generates short video clips or images for TikTok or Instagram. With literacy, the creator labels content as AI-generated, double-checks plausibility, and avoids presenting manipulated media as fact.

Without literacy, the same tool becomes harmful. A fabricated clip, posted without context, can circulate as breaking news. The difference lies not in the technology but in how responsibly it is applied. Applying literacy means embedding AI into creation and consumption with awareness of safety, truth, and impact.

Evaluating

Critical evaluation sits at the heart of literacy. The viral AI-generated image of the Pope in a white puffer jacket fooled millions because it looked plausible at a glance. [23] Evaluation means pausing before sharing, asking whether something is fact or opinion, and checking reliable sources. It is the difference between amplifying misinformation and resisting it.

To illustrate this dynamic, consider why false news often outpaces truth.

Deep Dive: Why Does False News Spread Faster Than Truth?

A well-known study of social platforms found that false stories travelled significantly faster than true ones. [24] Four drivers stand out:

|1 **Emotional triggers.** False news is designed to shock, surprise, or outrage. These emotions drive clicks and shares more effectively than neutral facts.

|2 **Novelty bias.** Humans are wired to pay attention to what is new, unusual, or counterintuitive. False news exploits this instinct.

|3 **Algorithmic amplification.** Engagement signals cause platforms to push provocative items to wider audiences.

|4 **Low barriers to creation.** It is easier to fabricate a striking image or headline than to verify facts.

A convincing image can outrun fact-checking. Literacy requires scepticism and deliberate pauses before sharing.

Creating

The highest level of literacy is not only about resisting manipulation but also about actively shaping how AI is used. A YouTuber who uses AI to stage fake headlines and then reveals the trick teaches audiences how to spot them. A TikTok creator who produces clearly labelled deepfakes as parody can educate viewers on the mechanics of deception. Newsrooms that experiment with AI can build transparent formats that show where AI assists and where human judgment remains essential.

Creating moves us beyond passive consumption. It turns literacy into a collective effort to strengthen our information ecosystems.

A Simple Maturity Model

These four dimensions can be visualised as a maturity model, combined and simplified from UNESCO, OECD, and EU DigComp sources:

+ **Starter.** Can explain AI in everyday language and use one or two tools.

+ **Practitioner.** Understands risks, applies strategies, and checks outputs.
+ **Leader.** Standardises practices, trains others, and integrates evaluation processes.
+ **Designer.** Co-designs AI systems, ensures governance, and aligns with ethics and compliance.

Deep Dive: Can ChatGPT Really Reason?

One of the most common questions about conversational AI is whether tools like ChatGPT actually reason. At first glance, they seem to. They can follow a chain of logic, debate trade-offs, and help structure research. What looks like reasoning is something different.

+ Humans reason by combining lived experience, abstract concepts, and logic, and by testing ideas against reality.
+ Large language models are trained on vast amounts of text to predict the next most likely word. They do not possess true understanding or self-awareness.

Why does it look convincing?

|1 **Training data.** Models absorb countless examples of human reasoning and can reproduce that style.

|2 **Emergent patterns.** At scale, outputs can simulate logical structure.

| 3 **Human interpretation.** We naturally project intentionality onto structured text.

When ChatGPT appears to do research or reason, it is retrieving and recombining patterns it has seen before, applying statistical shortcuts, and presenting them in a human-like format. It cannot independently verify truth, check sources, or generate new concepts from first principles. Which is precisely why literacy matters. Conversational AI is a powerful collaborator for brainstorming, summarising, and simulating reasoning, but responsibility for accuracy and logic remains with us.

Why AI Literacy Is a Survival Skill

Just as reading and writing once determined who could participate in society, AI literacy now shapes who thrives in the 2020s. It is not optional. People use generative tools daily, often without training or guardrails. Sensitive data is pasted into public models. Decisions are made on unchecked outputs.

AI literacy is not about mastering a single tool. It is the capacity to adapt, question, and evaluate in a fast-changing landscape. Literate users are more productive and, more importantly, less likely to be manipulated, blindsided, or left behind.

Playful methods help. Games such as Fakey or Bad News simulate social feeds and ask players to decide what to share, ignore, or fact-check [25]. They make manipulation visible and train scepticism as a reflex.

In Syntea, we use similar ideas. Short, TikTok-inspired micro-learnings deliver quick, engaging literacy moments in everyday workflows. If virality mechanics can spread misinformation, they can also spread competence.

A simple checklist also goes a long way. Before trusting an AI output, ask:

| 1 Is it fact or opinion?

| 2 What is the source?

| 3 Can I detect bias?

| 4 What is the likely purpose: inform, persuade, or manipulate?

| 5 Is the context current and relevant?

Five questions. Simple, memorable, and powerful.

The Human Side of AI Transformation

Technology is rarely the hardest part of transformation. People are. When we piloted Syntea, reactions varied. Some were excited: "Finally, I can save time." Others resisted: "This will replace me." One manager admitted quietly: "I do not even know how to use ChatGPT myself. How can I lead my team?"

That vulnerability reminded me of my own career shifts. At TikTok, I was not an imposter, but I had to learn quickly about creators and the relationships they formed with peers and fans. Earlier, when I left acting for product management at Rocket Internet, I did feel like an imposter. I was new to the world of investors, metrics, and technical decision-making. What saved me were bosses who believed in me and colleagues who acted as sparring partners. I learned to speak the language of both engineers and investors.

The lesson holds today. AI transformation is not about knowing everything. It is about creating cultures where people can admit what they do not know, learn together, and practice curiosity without fear.

Actionable Takeaways

For creators, audiences, educators, and community leaders:

| 1 Treat AI literacy like financial literacy. It is not optional. Build it into learning and daily practice.

| 2 Do not repeat the mistakes of viral platforms. Speed and engagement without oversight create chaos. Add context and governance early.

| 3 Use global frameworks. OECD and UNESCO dimensions are practical scaffolds, not academic abstractions.

|4 Lead with vulnerability. Admit what you do not know. Invite others to learn alongside you.

Closing

The bridge between TikTok and AI in everyday information life may seem unlikely. Both are shaped by the same forces: algorithms, attention, and human behaviour. The question is whether we will let those forces control us or build the literacy to control them.

From the outside, AI literacy may look like a niche topic. In reality, it belongs at the centre of every leadership discussion. When I sit in those boardrooms, I will make the case clearly: without AI literacy, businesses will struggle, employees will burn out, and societies will fracture under misinformation. With it, we can adapt, compete, and thrive.

Personal Reflection: From Virality to Value

Working across both the creator economy and AI-driven learning has shown me how closely media literacy and AI literacy are connected. At TikTok, I learned how attention behaves in real time and how creativity, timing, and authenticity can move millions within seconds. I also saw how authenticity and manipulation coexist. To navigate that space consciously, you need media literacy: the ability to understand who creates content, what motivates them, and how the platform itself shapes what we see.

With Syntea Learn+, the challenge feels different but related. We are again at the intersection of human behavior and technology, only this time it's not with the attention economy, but with the artificial intelligence economy. Generative AI is redefining how we create, communicate, and learn. It automates tasks, amplifies voices, and accelerates creativity. Yet, it also floods our feeds with synthetic content that often looks indistinguishable from the real. The same systems that help us produce more knowledge can also distort our perception of it.

For me, this is the reason why the bridge between media literacy and AI literacy matters deeply. One helps us interpret influence; the other helps us navigate artificial intelligence. Together, they form a critical literacy for the 21st century: a mindset that combines curiosity with discernment.

Technology will continue to move faster than most institutions. Platforms will rise and fade. Models will evolve. The challenge is no longer just to keep up, but to stay aware.

ABOUT THE AUTHOR

Dr Marina Economidou helps businesses hire top talent and professionals land career-defining roles in IT, AI, data, product, project management, change, and digital marketing. She delivers consulting projects from strategy to delivery, leveraging market insights and data-driven strategies to match the right people with the right roles.

| 15 |

Women Leaders Driving AI in the Workplace

Artificial intelligence is no longer futuristic—it's the backbone of today's global economy. From personalized recommendations on streaming services to the logistics systems that keep shelves stocked, AI powers much of what is taken for granted. Yet behind these systems are leaders shaping not just the technology, but how it is deployed, understood, and trusted. Among them, women are increasingly defining the future of AI with a blend of vision, ethics, and measurable impact.

Though women currently represent less than a quarter of AI professionals worldwide, those who lead in this space are transforming workplaces and industries alike. In critical roles across enterprise software, healthcare, robotics, and generative AI, women are building systems that are safer, more ethical, and drive commercial value. They are not merely participating in the AI revolution—they are architecting its future [26].

Architects of Innovation and Ethics

High-profile women in AI set a strategic tone for the industry, proving that the most impactful innovation is grounded in principle.

Mira Murati, former Chief Technology Officer at OpenAI, exemplifies this new era. Beyond steering product development for ChatGPT, she drives global dialogue around the ethical and societal dimensions of generative AI. Similarly, Daniela Amodei, co-founder and president of Anthropic, is a pioneer of "Constitutional AI," creating models with transparent, principled guidelines.

These leaders show that innovation and ethics are inseparable. Technical expertise alone is not enough; guiding organizations and society through responsible adoption is now the greater challenge.

Practical Takeaway:

Prioritize ethics alongside technical excellence. Embed principles like transparency, fairness, and accountability in projects from the start to achieve sustainable innovation [30].

Traits of Successful AI Leaders

Through my work as Senior Client Partner with dozens of organizations across logistics, retail, manufacturing, technology, and energy, I've witnessed firsthand the distinctive qualities driving successful AI transformation. While headlines focus on a few public figures, the quiet leaders—often women—deliver the real, practical change inside businesses.

Most effective AI leaders consistently demonstrate:

- **Translational Mindset:** They translate complex AI capabilities into clear business value for executives, teams, and clients.
- **Ethical Pragmatism:** They embed responsible practices—transparent data lineage, explainable models—ensuring AI is both trustworthy and commercially practical.
- **Boundary Spanning:** They integrate AI teams with business units, breaking silos to solve real-world, not theoretical, problems.

A powerful example: an operational leader in a global warehouse who mandated rigorous ROI tracking and led efforts to reskill staff as automation transformed roles. This pragmatism combined with human-centred thinking exemplifies successful AI leadership.

Practical Takeaway

Recruit, promote, and emulate leaders who translate AI into business value, bridge silos, and hold ethics central to their work. Companies that measure AI impact systematically outperform those that do not [27].

Bridging Technology and Industry

AI achieves the greatest value when applied to large, real-world challenges. Daphne Koller, co-founder and CEO of Insitro, has transformed drug discovery into a data-centric process, accelerating the development of life-saving treatments. Cassie Kozyrkov, Chief Decision Scientist at Google, champions "decision intelligence," making AI accessible and actionable for every level of the organization.

The most successful leaders:

- Translate technological innovation into business results.
- Anticipate adoption challenges, clarify ROI, and foster team unity.
- Combine technical, ethical, and strategic skills to set their teams apart.

Practical Takeaway:

Start every project by defining clear business outcomes. Align technology with these objectives and build cross-functional teams that bridge disciplines. Structured approaches like IBM's AI Ladder can help ensure successful adoption [28].

Powering the World's Backbone

AI is deeply embedded in systems that sustain global business, and women are leading these transformations.

In enterprise technology, Clara Shih at Salesforce AI enables companies to better understand customers and streamline operations. At SAP, leaders like Anja Schneider and Maryann Abbajay drive massive digital transformation efforts—proving AI adoption is about culture, not just code.

In logistics and manufacturing, Oana Jinga of Dexory reimagines the warehouse as an intelligent ecosystem, while Peggy Gulick at General Motors integrates AI into manufacturing for greater safety and performance.

Practical Takeaway:

Champion a culture of continuous learning and change within operations. Focus on measurable, practical value—efficiency, safety, profitability—at every implementation stage.

Global Voices and Inclusive Leadership

Women's leadership in AI extends far beyond Silicon Valley, focusing on inclusivity and regional impact.

In Africa, Zindi (co-founded by Celina Lee) deploys AI competitions to solve agricultural and community challenges.

In India, NASSCOM president Debjani Ghosh leads societal initiatives ensuring AI delivers value to the many, not the few.

These leaders prove that diversity—in culture, experience, and thought—is essential for building AI that solves global problems. Inclusive teams are 35% more likely to outperform financially [29].

Practical Takeaway:

Seek and promote diverse perspectives. Inclusive teams build solutions that earn greater trust and deliver broader, more relevant impact.

Hiring for AI Success—Practices to Cut Through Noise

As AI becomes a baseline skill in many roles, hiring leaders must move beyond buzzwords to genuine capability. Evidence of accountability, ethical grounding, and business translation are more predictive of success than technical credentials alone.

Instead of asking:

"What models did you train?"

Ask:

"Walk through how you delivered an AI project to a non-technical executive."

This tests both technical and translational skills.

Instead of asking:

"What algorithms did you use?"

Ask:

"Describe an AI failure in production. How did you assess business and ethical impact, and what governance measures did you implement?"

This evaluates ethical pragmatism and sustainable thinking.

Practical Takeaway

Design interviews and evaluations around real-world impact, business alignment, and ethical accountability—not just technical proficiency. Scenario-based evaluation aligns with best practices outlined in Deloitte's Responsible AI framework [30].

Lessons from Women Leaders

Across industries, women shaping AI share three defining qualities:

1. Visionary Thinking: They see AI as a transformative force for business and society.
2. Ethical Grounding: They embed transparency and fairness from day one.

| 3 Strategic Impact: They deliver measurable outcomes while shaping positive cultures.

These traits explain why women leaders excel at scaling AI responsibly and effectively across organizations.

Practical Takeaway:

Embed vision, ethics, and impact into leadership development and AI project planning.

A Blueprint for the Future

Today's women AI leaders are more than industry icons—they are defining the blueprint for the next generation of technologists. Their stories challenge the notion that AI is a male-dominated field and spotlight the necessity of diverse perspectives when shaping technologies that reach every corner of life.

If AI is to define the 21st century, its architects must reflect the world's diversity. The successes and lessons of these leaders demonstrate that innovation and responsibility aren't just compatible—they're mutually reinforcing.

Practical Takeaway:

Commit to diversity in hiring, leadership, and project teams to build AI systems that are ethical, effective, and globally relevant.

Personal Reflection: The Turning Point

If I had to pinpoint the single moment that shaped my approach to leading transformation through data and AI, it wouldn't be a massive project win. It was a failure of imagination—specifically, my own—early in my career.

I was working with a global supply chain client on a project to optimize warehouse staffing using predictive analytics. The models were beautiful: 99.8% accurate in forecasting daily labor needs, promising millions in savings. We presented the results with great pride.

The CEO listened politely, then asked one question that stopped me: "What happens to the 300 employees whose jobs your perfect model says we no longer need? Did you model that? Did you build a plan for them?"

My answer was technical. The CEO shook his head. "Your model is 100% right on the what, but 100% wrong on the how and the who. You've optimized the process, but broken the organization's trust. AI is a tool, not a decision. We don't run a business of algorithms; we run a business of people."

That moment was a searing lesson in Ethical Pragmatism and Boundary Spanning. I realized my technical expertise created a blind spot. My job wasn't just to deliver the most accurate algorithm; it was to deliver the most valuable, humane, and sustainable business outcome.

From that day forward, every AI or data project I've championed globally—whether in financial services risk, tech development, or logistics—has started not with the data, but with the human contract. It's why I insist on questions like: What is the re-skilling plan? How will we explain this decision to the end-user? What is the fail-safe if the model is biased?

This initial failure taught me that true leadership in AI isn't about technical dominance; it's about visionary empathy. It's about building a bridge between the precision of the machine and the complexity of human life—a perspective reflected every day in women leaders responsibly architecting the future of our industries.

ABOUT THE AUTHOR

Elisavet Kyritsi is a technology leader with nearly two decades of experience across GitHub, Microsoft, and Teradata. She builds ecosystems that connect innovation with people, driving AI adoption through collaboration and trust. Currently a Partner Development Manager at GitHub for EMEA, she focuses on empowering teams to grow through purpose and partnership. An MBA graduate from Imperial College London, Elisavet is passionate about mentoring and helping others navigate the intersection of technology, leadership, and change.

Elisavet Kyritsi, MBA

| 16 |

Leading Through Shifts in AI While Raising a Family Abroad

I come from Greece, a country that gave me strong roots. I grew up with a deep respect for education and close family ties. Yet, I also saw firsthand the barriers women in tech face when aspiring to leadership.

For the past sixteen years, I have lived and worked abroad, building a career in technology while raising two children, now seven and nine.

My path has moved alongside waves of technological change: from learning the basics of tech, to witnessing the first breakthroughs in human-interacting AI, to building trust in new technologies through security, to showing why data is the soil of AI. Today, my focus is on encouraging entire organisations to adapt modern practices and guiding them through digital transformation. Alongside these shifts, I have carried another important role—being a mother, balancing bedtime stories with late-night calls.

Mid-Career: Discovering the First Paradigm Shift

Around the midpoint of my career, I found myself at the centre of a major technological shift: the rise of conversational agents.

It was the first time AI felt less like a theory and more like something people could interact with. The idea that a system could talk back in a human-like way was revolutionary—and uncomfortable for many.

To help people imagine it, we even created business cards for these "virtual agents," giving them a seat at the organisation as if they were colleagues. It may sound odd now, but at the time it was necessary. Companies weren't just adopting software; they were adopting a new way of working.

That period taught me one of my most important lessons: **technology only moves forward when people can imagine it.** My role was not simply to deliver a product but to help people cross the psychological bridge toward a new reality.

Building Trust Through Security

Later, I worked in a context where security became central. Digital transformation was accelerating, but people would not modernize unless they believed their data was safe.

I saw how fear—of breaches, of losing control, of reputational damage, could block innovation. My work became about reducing that fear: creating communities, building transparency, and making safeguards clear.

That was when I learned that **trust is the invisible architecture of AI adoption**. Without it, nothing scales.

But trust is not built once; it is tested every day. The job is difficult because resistance, readiness, and even socioeconomic uncertainty all shape how people perceive new ideas. When the world around us moves too fast, we instinctively seek security —and sometimes that resistance is not to the technology itself, but to the pace of change.

In one role, there was significant overlap between my work and another team's, leading to friction despite an abundance of work for everyone. At first, this tension felt personal. But when we focused on shared outcomes, we slowly rebuilt alignment. It was only **after** delivering results together that real trust emerged. I realised then that trust enables collaboration even when structures or roles overlap. It is what allows people to come together despite external pressures and internal uncertainty.

Data as the Soil of AI

As AI matured, I moved into roles focused on data and analytics. It became clear that AI is not magic—it is only as good as the data beneath it.

If the data is incomplete or messy, AI cannot deliver. But with robust analytics, strong data platforms, and cloud foundations, AI becomes practical and powerful.

I came to see data as the soil that makes AI grow. Before you harvest, you must cultivate. This part of my journey taught me patience, discipline, and why it is important to have a solid foundation before making big promises.

A Challenging Moment: COVID and Asking for Help

One of the most difficult moments of my career came during COVID. My children were just two and four, home with me every day. At the same time, I was leading a critical project built on brand-new products—and it was not going well.

I tried to hold everything together, refusing to admit how much I was struggling. I feared that asking for help would make me look weak or like a failure.

Eventually, I had no choice. I opened up about the challenges and was paired with a more experienced colleague to co-lead the project. At first, I felt my authority slipping away. But slowly, I realised the truth: **leadership is not about doing everything alone.** It is about shaping the vision, guiding the plan, and accepting support when needed.

The project succeeded in the end—not because I carried it myself, but because I let go of the fear of appearing vulnerable. I learned that **knowing when to ask for help is leadership.**

It took me years to learn that lesson fully. I used to see asking for help as a weakness, until I realised that silence often makes problems grow. You need to identify the kind of obstacles others can truly remove—and when unsure, be transparent during check-ins about how a critical project is going. Asking early is not a failure; it is a sign of courage and trust in your team.

Building Ecosystems Today

Today, my work focuses on building ecosystems that can thrive in a rapidly evolving landscape—bringing together partners, teams, and communities, especially across diverse regions. I cannot control these organisations, but I can inspire them.

What works is not pressure but fairness. I show what is possible, celebrate small wins, and create environments where everyone feels they have a chance to succeed.

Across EMEA, I have witnessed how AI adoption varies by country. In some markets, readiness and curiosity are high; in others, economic uncertainty or language barriers slow things down. To drive transformation, I often need to translate messages—not just linguistically, but culturally. This is where **local partners** make all the difference. The criteria for collaboration are not limited to technological maturity, but include **deep market knowledge, language fluency, and cultural empathy.** That combination determines whether AI becomes real for people who might otherwise see it as distant or intimidating.

In one region, a small consultancy built its very first AI prototype. By sharing their story widely, I saw others gain courage: *If they can do it, so can we.*

This is how I lead now—not by holding power, but by sharing it. And that is where inclusion becomes the true engine of ecosystem success. Inclusion is not only about representation; it is about relationships. Ecosystems thrive when knowledge, experiences, and cultural perspectives are shared. The more diverse the circle, the more resilient and innovative it becomes. Inclusion fuels trust, and trust fuels transformation.

Politics and Belief in a Strong Europe

At one point, my path even took me into politics. I stood as a candidate in the European elections, driven by my belief that Europe must be strong and united if it wants to shape the future of AI.

This was not about personal ambition. It was about responsibility. I had seen how technology was reshaping societies, and I believed that Europe should protect inclusion, privacy, and human rights while competing globally in innovation.

Politics was harder than any corporate role—exposed, raw, unforgiving. But it gave me resilience and courage. Even though I did not win, I showed my children that standing up for your values matters, even when the result is uncertain.

Teaching My Children About AI and Work

My children see me constantly on the phone or traveling. Instead of hiding it, I explain it: "I am going to another country to help people succeed with AI," or "I'm traveling because I want to show others how to use new tools in a fair way."

Being transparent makes them feel part of my journey. And when I return, I am fully back. I leave the phone aside, go to basketball practice, and read bedtime stories. That rhythm—transparency when I leave, presence when I return—helps them accept my work and helps me keep balance.

Sometimes they even challenge me. Once, they asked: "Mama, do you love work more than us?" It was a question that cut straight to the heart. I told them: "My work and your father are like my fingers—if you cut one, I will hurt. But you, my children, are my thumbs. Without you, nothing works. You are essential."

That metaphor seemed to make sense to them. And to me, it is the truth. Work is important, but my children are what give me the strength and balance to do it.

And sometimes, they even teach me. My daughter once asked, "Why do people need help with AI?" Her question reminded me that if I cannot explain my work simply, then I may not be explaining it well enough to anyone.

Inclusion as My Compass

Across all these chapters—conversational AI, security, data, ecosystems, politics, and parenting—one principle runs through: inclusion.

I have seen how bias creeps into AI. I have seen how access to transformation is not distributed equally. I have seen how smaller players get left behind when only the big ones are supported.

For me, fairness and inclusion are not optional extras—they are my compass. Everyone deserves a seat at the table. And as a mother, I want my children to see that inclusion is something you live, not just something you talk about.

Lessons From the Journey

Looking back, there are a few lessons I carry with me:

- **Technology moves forward when people can imagine it.**
- **Trust is the foundation of transformation.** It takes time, honesty, and shared results. In a world of constant change and competing pressures, trust holds teams and ecosystems together.
- **Data is the soil of AI.**
- **Inclusion is the engine behind ecosystem success.** Ecosystems thrive when people from different backgrounds and cultures collaborate openly, turning diversity into shared growth.
- **Politics needs people who understand AI and have the courage to act.**
- **Knowing when to ask for help is leadership.** Vulnerability, transparency, and early communication save projects—and people.
- Balance is about rhythm, not perfection.
- Children are our compass. If they understand, the world will too.

Personal Reflection – Between Two Worlds

One evening, after a long day of meetings, I was cooking dinner while still on a call. My son tugged at my sleeve:

"Mama, can you be finished now?" At the same time, someone on the call was asking me how to motivate hesitant leaders.

I ended the call quickly and sat with him. Later, I explained why I was busy. He listened carefully and said, "So you help people be less afraid of AI?"

His words stayed with me. That is exactly what I do. Whether with ecosystems, with citizens in Europe, or with my own children, my role is to remove fear, build trust, and make new ideas less intimidating.

And maybe that is the essence of leadership in this AI era: being human enough to admit the struggle, strong enough to carry both roles, and honest enough to guide others—partners, communities, and even our children—through the unknown.

PART V: THE EDGE OF UNDERSTANDING

Personal clarity and resilience in a field evolving faster than we can describe.

ABOUT THE AUTHOR

Sanaz Jamalzadeh holds a Ph.D. from the University of Helsinki and is currently a Project Manager, specializing in artificial intelligence and digital health. She supports organizations across Europe in achieving impact through innovative AI and healthcare projects, co-creating new solutions that drive real-world value. With over eight years of experience in AI model development across sectors such as finance, healthcare, and pharmaceuticals, her expertise spans AI adoption, multimodal data integration, and generative AI development.

Sanaz Jamalzadeh, PhD

| 17 |

Learning and Innovating with AI in Medicine and Healthcare

We have lived through two clear waves of AI in health and life sciences. The first gathered pace in the mid-2010s as deep learning moved from computer vision into radiology and pathology, raising expectations about image reading and biomarker discovery. The second began in late 2022 when generative and multimodal models entered everyday use, making it easier to draft clinical notes, connect imaging with multi-omics, and even propose candidate molecules for discovery programs. The promise is real, and the opportunity has always been practical and urgent. Speeding up the research with AI, turning complex data into decisions that patients, researchers, and healthcare professionals can trust.

Stepping out of Mathematics and into the Clinics and Hospitals

As the tools matured, the question became simple: where could I help turn all of this promise into decisions that matter for real patients? The answer, for me, started with Machine Learning (ML) and led straight into clinics and hospitals. I began in Mathematics with a strong grounding in algorithms, and that base carried me naturally into ML and AI. I wanted to see results that reached real patients, so I focused on cancer research and the life sciences, where evidence is dense, and choices are consequential. Working with this data let me build models that made a visible difference in care, and I could see the benefits for patients as the work advanced. That was the moment when AI felt less like a concept and more like a tool for impact.

Working side by side with pathologists and oncologists in European hospitals, I built ML systems that learned from thousands of whole-slide images and helped services move faster. The models pre-screened large backlogs, highlighted regions that deserved attention, and turned long stretches of manual review into shorter, more focused confirmations so specialists could spend time on the hardest cases. The real shift came when image-derived features were linked with the rest of the chart, because connecting pathology patterns with clinical variables, therapies, and omics data turned pixels into patient-level evidence that teams could use. For selected cohorts, we added multi-omics profiles, and that integration via advanced AI approaches revealed signatures that tracked resistance and response in ways that clinicians could recognize during case discussions. These models did not replace judgment, yet they consistently surfaced biomarkers and molecular signals that matched what labs later confirmed. The result was a workflow that saved time, reduced rework, and gave pathologists a clearer line of sight from patterns on a slide to actions for a patient, and it showed how advanced AI can guide choices when it draws strength from both images and clinical context.

The most important achievement people associate with my career in this field is not a publication or a metric; it is that I learned how to win trust across the room among pathologists, clinicians, and computational biologists, around the output of ML and AI systems. I did not try to make anyone 'like' AI; I changed how we presented and verified the work. When a model flagged risk or a likely treatment response, I began with biology, not the accuracy or sensitivity numbers. I told the story the signal suggested, showed where that story could fail, and spelled out what evidence would change my mind. Bit by bit, the black box became a glass box you could interrogate, and the conversation shifted from 'Do we trust the model?' to 'Under what conditions is this useful?

Reproducibility and explainability remain the gating factors for adoption in digital health and precision medicine. If you cannot reproduce a result across scanners, stains, or sites and cannot explain why a patient-level decision was made, you will not get past the boardroom or the bedside.

From numbers on paper to the molecular tumor boards – a concrete win

As I moved from models on a screen to work inside hospitals, the goal became very clear. There is a lot of data sitting in databases, and there are real people waiting for insights that could change their treatment. The point was never to chase the best metric. It was to understand why some cancers resist therapy, to spot biomarkers worth testing, and to surface drug targets that clinicians could discuss in the molecular tumor board. Once a model's output entered that room, it stopped being "my result." It became a shared hypothesis that had to stand up to questions from oncologists, counter-examples from pathologists, and close reading from the computational team. These meetings bring everything together, patient history, images, genomics, and the latest evidence, and more of them are now digital so decisions are traceable and faster. In that setting, AI is not an oracle. It is a colleague who has to show his work.

In one collaboration, our models pointed to biomarker panels that seemed tied to treatment resistance. They were not definitive answers, but they gave clinicians new ideas that shaped trial screening and refined the next questions to ask. The real impact only struck me much later, when I met a patient whose therapy had been chosen with help from those AI models. It was no longer abstract lines of code or a debate on a tumor board; it was a person, alive and receiving care, because of work that initiated in our pipeline. That moment made the impact unmistakable: from code to a life changed.

From trials to the real world: when AI meets access and reimbursement

A second turning point in my career came when I took the same rigor to real-world evidence (RWE) studies in collaboration with pharmaceutical partners. We asked practical questions: How effective is this therapy outside trial criteria? Which co-factors shape outcomes? Can we predict who benefits or who harms? Those analyses do not just shape R&D. In Europe, they increasingly shape market access and reimbursement strategies. The policy landscape sharpened in 2025 as the EU Health Technology Assessment Regulation began joint clinical assessments for new cancer medicines and all advanced therapy medicinal products, with expansion planned in the following years to other products and selected devices. During the same period, the EMA and the FDA clarified how real-world evidence can inform regulatory and Health Technology Assessment decisions, which raised expectations for data quality, study design, and transparency.

In this environment, ML and AI become the link between hospital data in Europe and decisions in pharmaceutical development. We used models to turn electronic health records and registries into actionable insight, identified feature patterns that help explain response and non-response in hematology and oncology, and estimated treatment effects with causal ML rather than relying on simple correlations. ML approaches here gained high attention in finding features affecting the outcome for each specific disease indication. These approaches also supported creating synthetic control arms from external, de-identified patient data, rather than by recruiting new patients for a traditional control group reproducing trial-like conclusions in several settings.

What GenAI is changing and what still matters most

Picking up from imaging, multi-omics, and AI, the next wave has been less about a single breakthrough and more about how generative, multimodal AI lets us work across modalities at once. Since late 2022, health and life-science teams have begun using foundation models that read pathology images, link them with genomic and proteomic profiles, and summarize longitudinal records in one pass. I then started leading projects that used generative, multimodal AI to connect those signals end-to-end. Multimodal and generative approaches do not just classify, they fuse signals to surface mechanisms and narrow to compact, testable signatures. I have been leading projects that make the trustworthy use of GenAI tangible in healthcare, building virtual assistants that patients and professionals can rely on. The goal is to have safe tools that reduce routine workload while keeping humans in the loop. In primary care, assistants draft and structure information so General Practitioners and nurses recover time they used to spend on documentation and follow-ups. In mental health, they support monitoring and psychoeducation with clear handoffs to clinicians, and in oncology, they help teams run quality-of-life check-ins and treatment-adherence prompts that feed back into care plans. The guardrails are as important as the features, so we align with emerging guidance and run local assurance tests to monitor drift, uncertainty, and usage. Early studies of ambient documentation and digital symptom monitoring point in the same direction. These tools can lighten the administrative load and strengthen patient-reported insight, but only when governance and evaluation are built in from the start.

GenAI in biomedical research is another important strand of progress, especially when data are scarce. We generate synthetic data to augment specific modalities in oncology and mental health, carefully benchmarking fidelity, privacy, and fitness-for-purpose, so researchers can prototype models, stress-test pipelines, and compare methods before touching live patient records. In image-heavy domains, diffusion and GAN-based augmentation improve robustness and help models generalize; in text-centric settings, curated synthetic notes support rare-event detection and cohort simulation. None of this replaces real data; it prepares models for them. Synthetic datasets can accelerate development and protect privacy, but they demand transparent evaluation and limits on where they are used in the decision chain. That is why in the projects I am leading, the teams document provenance, release reproducible code and data dictionaries, and treat synthetic generation as an auditable step in the research workflow.

AI agents in Healthcare and Medicine

While biomedical and life science research is often centered on understanding disease at the molecular or cellular level, healthcare delivery focuses on treating human patients in all their complexity. In the work I am currently focusing on, we follow this approach: not a single all-purpose model, but a coordinated set of specialized AI agents working together to share the load across diagnostics, scheduling, billing, and treatment planning. AI agents in healthcare tend to fall into two broad categories based on their function. Clinical agents deal directly with patient care. They might diagnose diseases from imaging data, interpret lab results, track treatment responses, or personalize drug recommendations based on genomic data. These agents are designed to support medical decisions with accuracy and timeliness, often processing more data than a human clinician could feasibly manage. On the other hand, operational agents handle the logistical and administrative side of healthcare. These include systems for appointment scheduling, care coordination, prior authorization with insurers, and patient communication. Though less glamorous than diagnostics, these tasks are vital to the smooth functioning of health systems. When operational agents work in tandem with clinical agents, they help create an end-to-end AI-driven ecosystem that can respond to both the medical and organizational needs of each patient's journey. These agents communicate in natural language and integrate seamlessly with existing healthcare workflows.

We are at the dawn of a new era where AI agents are no longer just analytical engines; they are becoming creative partners in the scientific and medical enterprise. Whether exploring uncharted territories in cell biology or navigating complex patient pathways in hospitals, AI agents offer not just speed, but insight. They complement human intuition with data-driven rigor, transforming how we understand biology and deliver care. The road ahead will require careful design, ethical foresight, and interdisciplinary collaboration. But the destination is promising: a future where science and medicine are co-created by humans and machines, working together not in competition, but in harmony.

Key takeaways for tomorrow

- **Start simple and act now:** You do not need all the answers to begin your journey in AI and Healthcare. Small steps with one patient, one project, or one decision create real momentum.
- **Use AI as an amplifier, not a replacement:** Let AI handle the heavy lifting, summarizing, connecting data, and drafting, but remember human oversight is always crucial to focus on insight and care.
- **Build with care and measure what matters:** Data quality, bias, privacy, and workflow fit are challenges, but not barriers when they are tackled deliberately.
- **Stay curious and collaborative:** Progress comes from exploration and iteration; this field rewards determination and openness to learn.

Personal Reflection

I started my Journey with mathematics, far from biology, oncology, or hematology, and for a long time that distance felt like a wall. What I did have was curiosity and a steady belief that numbers, used well, could help people. Machine learning became the bridge, letting me carry the logic I loved into rooms where lives were being discussed. I wanted to work in medicine since I was at school, but I hoped to contribute without spending years memorizing genomics or biology before I could be useful. When I found AI, a door opened. I could learn the biology I needed step by step while building tools that made a difference. The real challenge was not the coursework; it was leaving the comfort of what I already did well. I had to accept being a beginner again, ask simple questions, and learn to speak across disciplines. Each time I did, the wall dropped a little lower.

There was another hurdle. Many meetings and panels in the field of AI were led by men, and sometimes the tone made it feel as if you had to prove you belonged before you could prove your point. I chose not to step back. I found allies, joined women-in-AI communities, and made a habit of bringing someone newer than me into the next room I entered. Mentoring became fuel. Telling younger women "You belong here, and your questions are assets" echoed back and strengthened my own voice.

The moment that still anchors me is not a prize or a headline; it is a conversation in a molecular tumor board where an AI signal turned into a shared hypothesis. I remember walking in with a result and walking out with a plan because clinicians, pathologists, and data scientists could all see why the signal might matter. That shift from "convince them" to "think together" is the work I am proudest of.

If there is a lesson in my path, it is simple. Impact does not require a perfect résumé. It asks for the courage to start, the humility to learn, and the discipline to build trust one decision at a time. This field is not waiting for the loudest voice; it is waiting for steady hands and clear minds. If you are curious and determined, step in. The path will meet you halfway.

ABOUT THE AUTHOR

Rosaline Pahud de Mortanges is Interim Head of AI, Data & Technology and founder of Dimensic. With 20+ years in IT, data, and strategic management, she builds AI solutions that simplify decisions and strengthen organizations. Her expertise spans data science and technical architecture. Passionate about data and sports, she also enjoys family life with her husband and two children.

Rosaline Pahud de Mortanges

| 18 |

Patterns that Matter in the AI ERA

Building a startup in Europe is different. We have strong communities and accelerator programs, but our ecosystem moves cautiously. We draft rules before pilots run. We ask what could go wrong before we identify what is needed now. That is careful, but the cost of waiting too long is irrelevance.

I write this as a female founder who has spoken with hundreds of organizations – from the work floor to the boardroom. My goal was never to "sell" a tool, but to uncover patterns: where things get stuck, which information is missing, which decisions remain unnecessarily blind. If you want to become better, you use data to measure.

While the rest of the world invests billions in intelligent systems, Europe hesitates. That hesitation is not only a technological lag; it is a risk of becoming irrelevant. Still, I don't believe Europe should simply move faster. Europe has a unique chance to move smarter. With our democratic values, public infrastructure, and scientific foundations, we can become a leader in purposeful AI: explainable, fair, and aligned with human judgment.

Patterns That Truly Matter

Many founders start by building a prototype. I chose another path. Instead of coding immediately, I wanted to understand what really drives processes inside organizations. That meant listening before building.

What I found is that problems are rarely "tool problems." They run deeper—in assumptions, outdated architecture, and blind spots in decision-making.

The assumptions are familiar:

- Processes work as designed.
- Decisions are made with full information.
- Teams see their own inefficiencies clearly.

The reality is different: legacy systems consume the budget, silos block information, and data quality is often unreliable. These aren't minor details. They are key drivers of whether AI succeeds or fails.

Seeing Differently – The Doctor and the Patient

Across industries, leaders act on assumptions. They trust experience, move quickly, and adapt— until something fails. Awareness is often missing. That is why I use a metaphor in my strategy sessions.

In these sessions, I ask participants to think as both doctor and patient:

|1 You have a heart condition, and surgery is necessary. Do you choose a manual procedure, or a robotic one that maps everything in advance and delivers better outcomes?

|2 Would you like to know if the robotic option even existed, or would you blindly trust the doctor?

|3 If transparency feels obvious in healthcare, why shouldn't employees and customers have the same clarity in decisions that affect them?

These are not theoretical questions. Imagine you truly experience this. Would you not think differently about governance, or about whether to apply AI at all? Perhaps it is the other way around: maybe you have a basic right to have those options offered. What now sparks fear – "should we use AI?" – may become tomorrow's standard. As in aviation, redundancy is not a luxury but a guarantee. If systems are designed to make decisions transparent, they build trust and improve outcomes, today and in the future.

I know this firsthand. I've always been sporty in my life, and unfortunately, I had extra systole in my heart rhythm. In my early thirties, as a new mother, I underwent a heart ablation. I was told it was routine. What I wasn't told: a robotic option existed, more precise and effective. The first attempt, manual, failed. The second, robotic, succeeded in thirty minutes. The difference was not only in the technology. It was in the awareness.

That's why I don't ask companies about tools, but about the patterns they overlook. A simple website request often reveals deeper goals: entering new markets, boosting sales, or improving collaboration. What they need is not a tool, but insight into their own situation – and how to improve it.

Inclusivity by Design – Lessons from Triathlon

When I completed my first Olympic triathlon, I realized how extraordinary it was that this sport had been inclusive from the very beginning. Where women in the marathon had to wait decades for recognition—Kathrine Switzer was almost dragged off the course in 1967, and only in 1984 did women get their Olympic place—in triathlon, women stood at the start line in Sydney 2000 alongside men.

Triathlon shows that new disciplines can create space without the burden of old restrictions. That is exactly the opportunity we have with AI. We can design inclusivity, explainability, and trust from the start, instead of forcing people to fight for it later.

Sport is not just physical. It's also about visibility, health, and ability to perform. Data in training, heart rate, recovery, and endurance make progress visible. That visibility builds confidence, strength, and resilience. The same is true for organizations. AI should not replace human judgment but make patterns visible, so decisions are stronger. For me, it is a powerful parallel with AI: we have the chance to design inclusivity and trust from the start, rather than forcing people to fight for it later.

The autonomous organisation – new technologies

As technologies evolve, the vision of my startup became clearer. Start building autonomous organisations. We started to build intelligent AI-agents designed not just to retrieve information, but to surface hidden patterns, safeguard redundancy, and make decisions traceable. By embedding knowledge management at the core, we ensure organizations don't just store information, challenge assumptions and act faster with confidence.

Agents are built on four principles: Decision-first, Early-warning, Explainable & Traceable, and Human-in-the-Loop, and become trusted copilots. Their power lies in knowledge management: creating a living hub where datasets, documents, and decision rules converge. With lifecycle retraining, strong security, and root cause traceability, agents evolve as the organization evolves.

This is the roadmap: map key drivers, prototype one trusted agent, embed governance first, measure wins, then scale with confidence. AI-agents are not gadgets if right developed.

Governance as Direction, Not Delay

AI governance isn't bureaucracy; it's the backbone of trust and security. The point isn't to slow teams down, but to make high-stakes decisions transparent, explainable, and safe before they scale. This is exactly what the European AI Act seeks to anchor: transparency, traceability, and accountability as foundations.

In practice, strong governance pairs these with rigorous security and lifecycle management: - Security by design: encryption, data minimization, zero-trust architectures, and least-privilege access.

|1 **Explainability & traceability:** every recommendation is linked to its inputs, rationale, model version, and data lineage.

|2 **Model & data lifecycle:** models and datasets are not static. Governance must include when to retrain, when to retire, and when to enrich models with new datasets. Outdated inputs can lead to flawed insights;

new data sources may require new licensing or introduce new risks.

|3 **Knowledge management:** ensuring that documents, datasets, and decision rules are stored, searchable, and reusable across projects. Without this, organizations repeat mistakes and fail to capture institutional learning.

|4 **Operational resilience:** fallback modes, canary releases, safe rollbacks, and incident response protocols so failures are contained. - Human oversight: material decisions remain subject to human approval, with escalation paths and periodic reviews against policy.

|5 **Trust is designed and maintained.** Done right, they turn knowledge into resilience, decisions into momentum, and momentum into sustainable impact. Waiting for certainty is a myth. The real risk is letting others build the systems you depend on. Start small. Start strong. But start today. Whether you are a retailer, municipality, logistics company, or healthcare provider, you are a data company. Perhaps you just haven't realized it yet.

The European Opportunity – Culture, Roles, and Courage

Europe has the world's first AI regulatory framework. Some see it as restrictive; I see it as a compass. What is missing is courage and investment. Where other countries scale rapidly, Europe waits. As a result, we often rely on foreign tools and weaken our own startups. AI is more than technology. Functions change, roles shift, andorganizations must learn to collaborate with intelligent systems. Success depends as much on culture and skills as on tools. I meet many companies full of ideas but hesitant to start with AI, still. The ones that thrive will use AI not to replace people but to strengthen them. What Europe needs is confidence in its own infrastructure – explainable, fair, scalable. Collaboration over hype. What we need is the confidence to use them.

From Insight to Action – A Checklist for Tomorrow

It is easy to get lost in the hype. But progress is not about adopting every new tool. It's about making conditions visible, so decisions become explainable and sustainable.

Most organizations spend most of their time reporting on the past: last month's KPIs, status updates, and after-the-fact analyses. Useful, but insufficient. The crucial question is not *what* we want to achieve, but *under which conditions* we will be sustainably successful. AI is not about predicting the future like a crystal ball, but about showing whether those conditions are present – or not.

Here is a simple checklist leaders can start with tomorrow:

Diagnosis

- What is our biggest blind spot?
- Which KPIs do we measure but not really understand?
- Which processes require redundancy and traceability?

Data & Systems

- Do silos block a single source of truth?
- Is most of our budget going to legacy maintenance?
- How do we ensure data quality and consistency?

Ways of Working

- Can employees query data in natural language?
- Is every management summary traceable to its source?
- Do we provide a safe sandbox for AI experimentation?

Governance & Security

- Are explainability, traceability, and redundancy required?
- Do we apply zero-trust access and clear lifecycle management?
- Is there an incident response and rollback plan?

Pilot

- Start with one process (e.g., quarterly reviews).
- Measure time saved, error reduction, decision quality.
- Scale only after repeatable success.

Takeaways:

|1 Map your key drivers—horizontally and vertically.

|2 Link data, systems, and people to those drivers. Start small, scale only after repeatable success.

|3 Design governance as direction, not delay.

|4 Use AI as a lens to reveal overlooked patterns.

Personal Reflection

My path into technology was not traditional. I grew up on board a ship, with parents who were shipowners navigating the rivers of Europe. At six I went to boarding school during the week, traveling back to the ship on weekends. That upbringing taught me resilience, adaptability, and the importance of systems that work under pressure.

From a young age, I taught myself programming, took courses, built prototypes, and worked for twenty years as a technical consultant in the maritime sector. I learned to spot patterns: systems that didn't connect, processes that drained energy, data that could not be trusted. Between 2018 and 2022, I immersed myself in data and AI, speaking with hundreds of companies. During Covid I learned more practical data science, with support of a professor from Indian University. Later, I complemented the CIO, CTO, and CDO Executive Program at Erasmus University in 2022-2023. That mix of practice and theory is my strength.

Sport has always been part of my life. Triathlon taught me that data makes progress visible, just as AI makes organizational blind spots visible. Both build confidence and resilience. My message is simple: there is no single path to impact technology or in life. Continuous learning, sharp observation, and the courage to build are the real conditions. AI is not the destination. It is the lens that helps us see. And if we want Europe to remain relevant, we must not wait for others to move. We must move smarter, start now.

ABOUT THE AUTHOR

Patricia Goodwin-Peters, DBA, is an accomplished Chief Human Resources Officer with over 25 years of experience driving transformation in complex, global organizations. Most recently, CHRO at Atlas Air Worldwide, she led strategic HR initiatives across 5,000+ employees worldwide. Patricia holds a Doctorate in Business Administration from the University of Florida, where her research explores how organizational systems enable or constrain HR's ability to deliver enterprise value.

| 19 |

The Human Advantage in the Age of Artificial Intelligence

From the moment of birth, a human being begins accumulating an endless constellation of interactions—each one shaping perception, stirring emotion, and imprinting meaning. Like crystals forming on a snowflake, no two are ever the same. This is human coding, layered through time, experience, and emotion. It cannot be replicated, downloaded, or scaled. It is rare, inimitable, and deeply valuable. In a world of algorithms and automation, humanity remains the greatest competitive advantage.

And yet, even as we celebrate what makes us human, we must also contend with a force that challenges it: artificial intelligence. It is no longer on the horizon—it is here, reshaping how organizations compete, innovate, and grow.

For many C-suite executives, the promise of AI has been tied to efficiency and scale—faster workflows, reduced headcount, increased productivity. Boards and CEOs are already pressing Human Resources and Technology leaders to deliver on these gains. But if implementation begins and ends with cost-cutting, organizations risk eroding one of their greatest assets: the uniquely human ideas, creativity, and relationships that no algorithm can replace.

For leaders, and especially for Human Resources, this is not just about adopting new tools. It is about reimagining how work gets done, how people thrive, and how culture endures in a rapidly changing landscape. AI can accelerate change, but it cannot define an organization's identity. Culture, creativity, trust, and belonging—the forces that truly differentiate companies—remain uniquely human. The opportunity for leadership and HR is not simply to adopt AI but to ensure its deployment strengthens rather than diminishes the very things that make organizations thrive.

The stakes are high. While the World Economic Forum projects a net gain of two million jobs globally by 2027, that growth will not be evenly distributed. Without foresight, the disappearance of entry-level and administrative roles may quietly dismantle the developmental infrastructure organizations need for the future. For decades, these roles have served as proving grounds, cultivating judgment and offering early glimpses into how organizations operate under pressure. If we eliminate them without replacing the purpose they served, we risk a future where fewer people know how to lead—and fewer still have the chance to learn.

We have been here before. During the blue-collar automation era, entire industries were upended. Some companies turned away, leaving workers and communities behind. Others leaned in—retraining employees, redesigning jobs, and investing in new pathways. Without deliberate investment in reskilling, rotational experiences, and redesigned roles that stretch people beyond task completion, we risk widening the gap between those who can adapt and those left behind.

But there is another lesson from history worth remembering. The first technology boom, fueled by the rise of personal computers, did not contract opportunity—it expanded it. Entire industries were born, new careers opened, and a generation of workers gained tools that multiplied their potential. That is the model we should aspire to now: using AI not to replace tasks, but to create new avenues for growth, innovation, and participation.

The lesson is clear: disruption without design leaves people behind. But when met with foresight, it creates opportunity—a chance to build something more resilient, equitable, and ultimately more human.

Ignoring the human component essential for AI introduces significant risk. AI's potential is extraordinary—but not infinite. Every insight, every innovation, every spark of "intelligence" originates with humans—our stories, creations, and connections. Without human imagination and lived experience, AI quickly reaches its limits. It cannot invent meaning; it can only rearrange what already exists.

The glorious experience of being human—our contradictions, emotions, and discoveries—is the lifeblood that fuels AI's evolution. Without imagination, AI stagnates. Without diverse perspectives, its insights are narrow. And without meaning, it loses purpose.

Human creativity, curiosity, and consciousness are not just valuable—they are essential. So why do we ignore them? And why aren't they a core part of the AI story?

AI needs us as much as we are beginning to lean on it. The future of innovation depends on this reciprocal exchange. The road ahead can be extraordinary. The question is: where do we begin?

Building a Harmonious Future: Where People and AI Align

We begin by bringing people into the process. Leaders must embrace AI as a strategy of **expansion, not contraction.** Doing so brings employees along in the most profound way, turning anxiety into curiosity and resistance into engagement. The implementation of AI is, at its core, another exercise in change management. Decades of research show that 33% to 80% of change initiatives fail—often not because of flawed technology, but because of unaddressed human dynamics (Coch & French, 1948). Any significant transformation, like the one that AI poses, can trigger a threat response: "Will this change my role? Will I still be valued? Will it be worth the effort?" As Strebel (1996) noted, employee resistance is rarely irrational—it stems from a misalignment between individual values and perceived organizational intentions.

I experienced this firsthand as a Chief Human Resources Officer leading an enterprise-wide transformation that involved implementing an AI-enabled platform to consolidate processes previously spread across multiple departments. The effort was positioned as part of our Value Creation Plan—a term employees immediately translated to "headcount cuts." Despite our strategic intent to streamline and empower, fear took root. The project stalled for months.

What became clear was this: resistance, when shared and unaddressed, becomes a collective force strong enough to halt even the most promising innovations.

We had to hit reset. Drawing on Servant Leadership principles (Greenleaf, 2002), we rebuilt the effort around trust and participation. We introduced foresight sessions to explore the "why" behind the changes. We leaned into persuasion—not mandates—and reframed the initiative not as a threat, but as a bridge to the future.

We acknowledged the loss that employees were feeling and responded with the introduction of tangible support, including teamwork workshops, transparent communication, celebration of wins, and a movement towards an internal academy focused on upskilling, mobility, and career resilience. We invited feedback, co-designed solutions, and most importantly, reinforced that no tool—AI included—should replace human dignity, ingenuity, or opportunity.

This reframing transformed the initiative. Employees who had once resisted began to champion the effort. Trust was rebuilt not through technology itself, but through how we chose to implement it.

For me, this experience was a powerful reminder: AI is not just a tech rollout—it is a cultural reckoning. And culture changes only when people feel seen, heard, and valued.

Where Leadership Must Meet Action

AI cannot transform an organization on its own. Even the most sophisticated rollout cannot address the human element—that responsibility belongs to leaders. It belongs to those willing to reimagine how value is created, how people contribute, and how systems evolve to support both. To realize AI's promise, leaders must take ownership of the human dimensions of transformation: trust, collaboration, and change.

This begins with a mindset shift.

Leaders must resist framing AI as a cost-cutting exercise. That approach is shortsighted. It delivers diminishing returns and assumes a fixed pie rather than expanding what is possible. Efficiency has its place—but real transformation demands something bolder, more expansive, and unmistakably human.

It starts not with answers, but with better questions:

- Which tasks can we automate to free time for more meaningful work?
- Where is human judgment essential—and how might AI enhance it?
- What new skills will redesigned roles require?
- How do we reshape workflows so people and machines complement each other?

Leaders who ask these questions—and invite their teams to help answer them—will not just implement AI; they will redefine their organizations, setting the tone for a culture of curiosity, agility, and shared purpose.

The future of work will not be built by eliminating people but by investing in them—by:

- Designing jobs that amplify uniquely human strengths
- Cultivating cultures where innovation lives on the front lines
- Shifting talent systems from rigid control to continuous growth

This is where HR must lead—and leadership must be willing to follow. HR must partner with the business to rearchitect job structures, identify emerging skill needs, and evolve learning strategies to meet the moment. Moving from static roles to skills-based models allows organizations to adapt with agility, align talent to business needs, and build a truly future-ready workforce.

Transformation at this scale requires more than vision. It demands executive ownership and a sustained commitment to reskilling—particularly for populations at highest risk of displacement. We cannot afford to lose the institutional knowledge often held in entry-level and administrative roles that have quietly powered success for decades.

Leaders must champion a broader view of talent development—one that extends beyond company walls. Organizations should re-evaluate learning strategies, identifying not just what needs to be learned but who must be included. This means building skills both inside and outside the company—partnering with schools, workforce boards, local governments, and nonprofits. There are scholarships, grants, and public-private collaborations waiting to be activated—but only if leadership steps forward to engage them.

This is not charity. It is a strategy. Those who lead in workforce development will shape the talent markets of tomorrow, while others are still reacting to the shocks of today.

Sustaining Competitive Advantage

The organizations that will define the next decade are not those that adopt AI the fastest, but those that integrate it most thoughtfully. Competitive advantage lives at the intersection of technology and humanity:

- Machines provide scale; humans provide meaning.
- Algorithms deliver speed; people bring judgment.

- AI powers insights; culture powers innovation.

Success depends on leadership's ability to align technology strategy with purpose. This is not just about deploying tools—it is about ensuring people, processes, and culture evolve together. Companies that integrate AI with the intention of fostering trust, collaboration, and innovation. Those that focus narrowly on efficiency risk eroding culture, disengaging employees, and losing the very talent they need to compete.

Leadership sets the vision; HR enables adaptability—equipping employees, preparing leaders, and ensuring culture evolves with capability. Sustaining advantage in the age of AI demands that people and technology advance together—not at each other's expense.

AI is here, and its impact is undeniable. The organizations that thrive will not treat it as a cost-cutting shortcut but as a catalyst for growth. They will design intentionally, lead transparently, and center people at every step. Because in the end, AI is not replacing us—it is reshaping the canvas on which we create value.

The future belongs to those who understand a simple truth: the real differentiator is not artificial intelligence—it is human intelligence, amplified. Leaders must embrace AI as a strategy of expansion, not contraction. Our job is not merely to protect people from change, but to help them see what change can make possible. Fear must be met with information; uncertainty with transparency; disruption with vision. When people believe they have a role in the future, they stop resisting it—and start building it.

This is not a time for incrementalism. It is a time to be as bold and imaginative as the technology itself—to reimagine roles, workflows, and outcomes that unlock the combined potential of people and machines.

For any executive shaping an AI strategy—CEO, CTO, CHRO, or Chief Transformation Officer—the path forward is clear:

- Ask your board: Do we want AI to deliver expansion or contraction?
- Embed workforce development: Make reskilling core to your roadmap—and your ROI.
- Frame AI not as a threat to culture, but as a catalyst for evolution.

The future is not something we step into—it is something we co-create, with vision, courage, and people at the center.

Closing Thought

This chapter was born of an intentional partnership—between human and machine, heart and code. As a Chief Human Resources Officer and writer, I brought the tone, the thematic direction, and the lived experience. I shaped the voice, selected the metaphors, and wove in the truths that only a human can feel. Generative AI stood beside me, not in front of me—offering clarity where my ideas were dense, structure where my thoughts stretched wide, and precision where language fell short.

Together, we created something more substantial than either of us could have produced alone. Not because the technology led, but because it listened, responded, and adapted—becoming an extension of my creative process. That is the future I believe in—a future where technology amplifies our thinking, honors our humanity, and reminds us that the rarest form of intelligence will always be the kind that feels.

Personal Reflection

From my earliest encounters with technology, I was captivated—not by the machines themselves, but by their quiet promise: to enable, to enhance, to empower. I vividly remember my first time using Microsoft Office, marveling at how Word, Excel, and PowerPoint expanded the horizon of what I could create on my own. Each wave of innovation since the internet, mobile technology, and data analytics—felt like adding a new brushstroke to a growing canvas of possibility. With every tool, I could connect more deeply, build more boldly, and contribute more meaningfully.

But the moment that reshaped my perspective came during the COVID-19 pandemic. Overnight, companies were thrust into an entirely virtual world. As a Chief Human Resources Officer, I had a front-row seat to the human impact of this transformation. We leaned hard on every digital resource at our disposal. At first glance, it was tempting to credit technology for the continuity—but beneath the surface, something more profound revealed itself.

The organizations that endured—some even flourished—were not those with the most sophisticated platforms, but those with the strongest bonds. Trust, collaboration, and shared purpose had been forged long before we learned the phrase "social distancing." Technology made remote work possible; human connection made it sustainable. Without that emotional infrastructure, no digital system would have been enough.

This experience deepened my conviction that while technology is a powerful enabler, it cannot replace what makes us exquisitely human: our imagination, our empathy, and our capacity to connect with others in ways no algorithm can emulate. As CHRO, I came to see more clearly that our role is not to shape people around tools, but to shape tools around people—to ensure that AI, analytics, and automation are used to elevate human potential, not reduce it.

For me, this is the enduring truth: ***technology without humanity is hollow.*** *The future of work will not be written by machines alone, but by leaders who know how to use them to build trust, inspire creativity, and cultivate environments where people thrive.*

ABOUT THE AUTHOR

Isaura Martinez is an AI Marketing & Customer Lifecycle Strategist with expertise in strategic communications and customer engagement. She advises businesses on using AI and emerging technologies to design scalable marketing systems, optimize retention, and integrate storytelling into growth strategies. Through her writing and coaching, she challenges professionals to rethink business and marketing, and to thrive in a rapidly evolving global marketplace shaped by AI.

| 20 |

Misfit Logic: Finding Your Voice at the Edge of AI

Back in 2022, when many dismissed this "AI thing" as temporary—just a fad or a stage—I felt differently. It was clear something bigger was happening. When I created my ChatGPT account in early December of that year, I knew Marketing would never be the same. Ever.

The very first thing I asked was: "*Write a blog about Marketing.*" In seconds, it delivered. It was thrilling—and a little terrifying. We were having real conversations with machines. When I told my dad about it, he compared it to *2001: A Space Odyssey*—humans talking to a computer through a screen. He was right. Decades later, we were finally living in that reality.

One of the biggest misconceptions about emerging technologies is thinking they only impact IT or engineering teams. In truth, developers use these tools to build solutions for problems across every area of business. And Marketing is no exception.

In a crowded, competitive landscape, companies need new ways to connect with their audiences, show the value of their solutions, and ultimately win customers. That requires time, money, and resources. Which is why marketers are turning to AI—to work smarter, move faster, and amplify results.

SurveyMonkey research from the first half of 2024 highlights the most common AI use cases in marketing:

- Content creation (social media, blog posts, slides, emails) – 50%
- Content optimization (SEO, email campaigns) – 51%
- Brainstorming – 45%
- Research – 40%
- Data analysis for insights – 41%
- Automating tasks and processes – 43%

And it doesn't stop there. A CoSchedule survey found that marketers using AI see huge benefits—scaling content, boosting efficiency, and reducing costs. No wonder 9 out of 10 marketing professionals plan to increase AI adoption in 2025 and beyond.

The world of work is changing, and marketers aren't about to get left behind. Why? Speaking from more than a decade of experience in B2B tech and eCommerce—doing everything from blogging and copywriting to CRM, email marketing,

SEO, and managing global, remote marketing teams—I've seen firsthand how quickly we adapt.

So here are my thoughts on how (and why) marketers are ready to take AI by storm—not just for the next few years, but for the decades ahead.

The Mindset Behind AI Adoption

In an in-person AI course, the teacher said something that stuck with me: "*Besides IT, Marketing people are the ones with the highest AI adoption within organizations.*" She didn't say it lightly. Her work involves guiding companies through digital transformation, helping teams integrate AI into their workflows to boost efficiency. That insight came directly from her experience.

As an early adopter myself—jumping into ChatGPT back in 2022 without being a "tech person"—I didn't think it was a big deal at first. Everyone seemed to be trying it, right? But when I brought it up in conversations, people looked at me like, "*Wait, what?*" It felt too strange, too futuristic, maybe even like a passing wave. Except I knew it wasn't. Something fundamental had shifted, and there was no going back.

So why are marketers leading the way in AI adoption? A few reasons stand out:

| 1 **Curiosity** – Marketers are naturally curious. We thrive on testing new ideas, experimenting with strategies,

and finding better ways to deliver results. It's practically our default mode.

|2 **Storytelling** – Marketing is all about storytelling. Writers tell stories with words, designers with visuals, analysts with data. AI doesn't replace this—it expands the possibilities, giving us new ways to craft and share stories.

|3 **Change & Adaptability** – Marketers are wired to embrace change. While others may resist until trends are proven, we're often the ones experimenting, innovating, and sometimes even leading these shifts within organizations.

When most people think of marketing, they picture social media reels, eye-catching visuals, or sharp blog posts. But marketing is much more than that—it's both art and science. And AI, in many ways, sits at the intersection of the two. The technology is powerful, yes—but how we apply it is the art.

Every marketer will find their own way of using AI. Beyond the common use cases, each of us is experimenting, adapting, and shaping unique practices that fit our own style, industries, and audiences. That's where the real magic happens.

A Brand's Voice in The Age of AI

When I first asked ChatGPT to write a blog about marketing, it was terrifying. The thought that kept circling in my head was:

How can this technology write in seconds what usually takes hours—or even days?

Beyond the obvious worry about what this meant for the future of writing (a debate still very much alive, with more questions than answers), another concern emerged: *What happens if every brand starts doing the same—writing the same and sounding the same?*

AI has undeniably transformed efficiency. Today, anyone can produce a blog post, a social media caption, an email campaign, or ad copy in seconds. But what began as AI's biggest strength could easily become its greatest weakness. Generating content quickly doesn't guarantee quality. Even with flawless grammar and syntax, it doesn't automatically connect with an audience.

And connection is everything. If automation makes every brand sound alike, everyone loses. Instead of being recognized as the solution to your customers' problems, your brand becomes part of the noise.

Standing out in a crowded market requires more than efficiency. It means understanding your audience's pain points, hopes, and expectations—and speaking to them in a voice they recognize. No product "sells itself." Tone matters just as much as the message. That's why AI shouldn't be seen as a replacement for marketers but as a partner—helping us connect more authentically, not less.

That's exactly what led me to build my first AI Copywriter, which I named **PatricIA**.

As a communications graduate—not a "tech person"—building technology always felt out of reach. I once told a friend, "*I wish I liked coding.*" For years, I felt excluded from the tech world because I couldn't *create* technology. Then I realized: technology is created for people, and my role has always been to translate it for them—to show how software and apps can serve their needs.

One of the greatest gifts of the AI age is that it lowers the barriers to creation. I love experimenting with AI assistants (or "agents") tailored for specific functions. The technology itself is often simple; what makes an assistant powerful is the system behind it—the prompt, the parameters, the logic that shape how it performs.

For years, I've helped clients define their brand voices using the **12 brand archetypes**—the Hero, Sage, Magician, Creator, Explorer, Rebel, Caregiver, Lover, Everyman, Jester, Ruler, and Innocent. The idea is simple: even if two companies sell the same product, they don't sell it *in the same way.* Different customers have different motivations, desires, fears, and expectations. Language has to match that. Every brand has a personality. Even in a crowded market, only *you* can sound like you.

That philosophy shaped how I built PatricIA. I've given limited access to people and received great feedback—both on its effectiveness and how to make it even better. And this is just the start. I'm now developing more AI assistants for Marketing and Sales, designed not only to save time but also to amplify results.

Personal Reflection - There's a Place for You. Claim It

For years, I asked myself why I hadn't pursued a technology degree. Surrounded by the excitement of new solutions and innovations, I often felt like I didn't belong. My lack of a tech background felt like a burden—even though I had chosen Communications out of passion for writing and creativity.

Was I betraying myself for wanting something different? Did I have to leave behind what I loved just to be part of these exciting "trends"?

Now, as the barriers to technology keep falling, I realize the answer is no. Instead of closing doors, this new era is opening them wider than ever. I get to expand my creative side—and it feels incredible. But what feels even better is knowing I finally have a seat at the table.

Every professional experimenting with AI today—while the context, rules, and best practices are still unclear—is shaping the future. We're not just waiting for others to define the path. We're writing the rules as we go.

If you're an early adopter, a pioneer, someone willing to embrace change and adapt along the way—your place is already there, waiting for you. It always has been.

Claim it.

REFERENCES

Notes

[1] IATA. 2021 Safety Report, Edition 58. IATA , Apr. 2022.

[2] MIT's GenAI Divide: State of AI in Business 2025 https://www.mckinsey.com/capabilities/transformation/our-insights/common-pitfalls-in-transformations-a-conversation-with-jon-garcia?utm_source=chatgpt.com

[3] Syed, Matthew. Black Box Thinking : Why Most People Never Learn from Their Mistakes--but Some Do. Portfolio Penguin, 2016.

[4] Elon University (2025). Survey: 52% of U.S. Adults Now Use AI Large Language Models like ChatGPT.

[5] Dealroom (2025). Building Tech Ecosystems: Transitioning to an AI-First Ecosystem.

[6] An API (Application Programming Interface) is a set of rules that allows one piece of software (the startup's application) to communicate with and request a service from another piece of software (like an external AI model). In AI-First businesses, the term "API call" often refers to a transaction, which is the direct source of consumption costs.

[7] A GPU cycle (Graphics Processing Unit cycle) is the fundamental unit of time and processing power required to run an AI model. Unlike traditional software, where marginal cost is near zero, every time an AI product generates a result, it consumes these cycles, turning customer usage directly into a real, non-linear expense (the "compute burn rate").

[8] When individuals use AI tools generally to enhance their work, without required IT security, or legal safeguards.

[9] https://digital-strategy.ec.europa.eu/en/policies/regulatory-framwork.ai

[10] https://digital-strategy.ec.europa.eu/en/policies/nis2-directive

[11] AI can improve privacy and cyber protections, including Privacy Enhancing Technologies (PETs): by classifying sensitive data; right to be forgotten improvements; and network monitoring/ flagging anomalies.

[12] Wholeheartedly recommend https://www.amazingif.com/ for insight into Squiggly Careers.

[13] The GenAI Divide: State of AI in Business 2025, https://nanda.media.mit.edu/

[14] AI projects failure rates on the rise: Report. (2025, March). CIO Dive.

https://www.ciodive.com/news/AI-project-fail-data-SPGlobal/742590/

[15] Decision intelligence market, https://ww.cervicornconsulting.com/decision-intelligence-market

[16] Polanyi, M. (1966). The tacit dimension. University of Chicago Press

[17] Kahneman, D. (2011). Thinking, fast and slow. Farrar, Straus and Giroux.

[18] The GenAI Divide: State of AI in Business 2025, https://nanda.media.mit.edu/ and amplify

[19] Clayton, A. (2023, May 22). Fake AI-generated image of explosion near Pentagon spreads on social media. The Guardian. https://www.theguardian.com/technology/2023/may/22/pentagon-ai generated-image-explosion

[20] European Commission. (2022). The Digital Competence Framework for Citizens (DigComp 2.2). Publications Office of the European Union. https://joint-research-centre.ec.europa.eu/projects and-activities/education-and-training/digital-transformation-education/digital-competence framework-citizens-digcomp/digcomp-framework_en

[21] OECD. (2025, May). Empowering learners for the age of AI. OECD Publishing.

https://ailiteracyframework.org/wp-content/uploads/2025/05/AILitFramework_ReviewDraft.pdf

[22] UNESCO. (2024). AI Competency Framework for Teachers. UNESCO Publishing. https://www.cedefop.europa.eu/en/tools/vet-toolkit-tackling-early-leaving/resources/unesco-ai competency-framework-teachers

[23] Vosoughi, S., Roy, D., & Aral, S. (2018). The spread of true and false news online. Science, 359(6380), 1146–1151. https://doi.org/10.1126/science.aap9559

[24] The New York Times. (2023, March 27). The AI-generated pope in a puffer jacket fooled us all. https://www.nytimes.com

[25] Roozenbeek, J., & van der Linden, S. (2019). Fake news game confers psychological resistance against online misinformation. Palgrave Communications, 5(65). https://doi.org/10.17863/CAM.41437

[26] OECD. (2023). OECD AI Principles. https://www.oecd.org/going-digital/ai/principles/

[27] Harvard Business Review. (2022). Measuring AI Impact for Business Results.

[28] IBM. (2022). AI Ladder Framework for Deployment.

[29] McKinsey & Company. (2020). Diversity Wins: How Inclusion Matters.

[30] Deloitte. (2021). Responsible AI Framework.

Made in United States
Cleveland, OH
18 March 2026